Walking in Two Worlds
WOMEN'S SPIRITUAL PATHS

To the Franciscan Sisters of Little Falls, Mn.

Janice Weniger

Walking in Two Worlds
WOMEN'S SPIRITUAL PATHS

Edited by
Kay Vander Vort
Joan H. Timmerman
Eleanor Lincoln

Joan Timmerman

Eleanor Lincoln, css

Kay Vander Vort

NORTH STAR PRESS OF ST. CLOUD, INC.

Library of Congress Cataloging-in-Publication Data

Walking in two worlds : women's spiritual paths / edited by Kay Vander Vort, Joan H. Timmerman, Eleanor Lincoln.
  208 p. 23 cm.
  Includes bibliographical references.
  ISBN: 0-87839-073-1 : $14.95
  1. Woman (Christian theology) I. Vander Vort, Kay, 1936-
II. Timmerman, Joan H. III. Lincoln, Eleanor.
BT704.W35 1992
208'.2—dc20   92-29064
                                                                     CIP

Cover art: Gertrud M. Nelson

Printed in the United States of America by Versa Press, Inc., East Peoria, Illinois.

Published by North Star Press of St. Cloud, Inc.
P.O. Box 451, St. Cloud, Minnesota 56302

ISBN: 0-87839-073-1

Dedicated to all women—
that their spiritual paths
may lead them to their deepest desire.

Contents

Foreword

Women always walk in two worlds. Born into the "Adam's world" of culture consistently "named" from male life-experience, we find ourselves with language and categories that do not fit or name our experience as girl children or female adolescents. We early come to know "girltruth," which is experience *without* a language.

If born into Christian households, we grow up with archetypes of Eve as sinner and Mary as obedient vessel, who loom over our personal symbolic universe. All our lives we struggle with unfriendly myth and androcentric language, struggle to reclaim our own authentic identity from those who would create us "in their own image."

Born into Western cultures and deeply steeped in these two symbolic icons of Eve and Mary, we find ourselves culturally declared inferior, second-class, submissive, our female bodies deeply suspect, intended by some implicit order of nature to live not for ourselves but vicariously for husband and children.

If being male in Adam's world means coping with a superinflated "hero" identity, and wondering daily why one is not so heroic, then being female in Adam's world means coping with a super-*de*flated "inferior" status, wondering daily how one reverses that stigmatized identity into authentic, empowered, woman-living. This is a struggle shared by people of color in a white-dominated culture.

Born into a body-denying Christian culture haunted by the image of woman as sexual temptress to sin, girls and women come to know their female bodies as profoundly ambiguous. Assumed to be heterosexual, bombarded by cultural images obsessed by thinness and big breasts and violence toward women, instructed to "Say No" and stay chaste yet treated as sex objects by men taught to feel contempt for women's bodies and to link sex with violence, told how to experience an orgasm by Freudian psychology, denied birth control and abortion by male clerics who themselves never conceive or gestate or give birth—how in such a context is a real, alive woman ever to come to know, love and honor her own body?

How can she appreciate her own breasts and vagina, her own clitoris and labia, her own ovaries and uterus? How can she be "norm" for her own experience? How can she find her own words and name herself and her own female body experience?

To walk in these two worlds—of patriarchal power and women's body/life experience—is to know confusion and silence, invisibility and wordlessness, pain and betrayal, yet amazing hope and renewal.

Adam's silent partner is waking up and finding words to express her "womantruth." Woman-experience is finally finding voice and language.

In this book the woman-experience of walking in two worlds finds powerful expression. The wrestling with myth and language in both church and culture; the journey of transition from old identity to new authenticity; the powerful feelings of anger and aloneness, power and ambiguity; the discovery of the feminine face of God; the discovery of the reality of women's body experience—all are shared boldly and poignantly and lucidly by these authors.

It is a special pleasure for me to introduce and celebrate this book, which has emerged from the dynamic process of the Theological Insights program based at The College of St. Catherine, because our own Theological Opportunities Program at Harvard Divinity School has been a point of origin for the program at St. Catherine's.

We are linked together by the passion for women "telling our own stories." We share the sure knowledge that women's "faith communities" such as we represent are vitally necessary to sustain and empower women today on our unique spiritual journeys.

Any reader of *Sacred Dimensions of Women's Experience* (created in 1988 out of the Theological Opportunities Program) will find in this book new companions for their journey. We in Boston rejoice with the Theological Insights program as they celebrate the latest flowering of their community in the publication of this book for their fifth anniversary.

Together we honor the historical moment of women's awakening, which has given birth to us both.

Elizabeth Dodson Gray
Wellesley, Massachusetts
1992

Introduction

"I feel I'm walking in two worlds." One woman's comment about her spiritual experience led to the question: "What worlds do women walk in?" In this book, *Walking in Two Worlds*, twenty-one women share their struggles of walking in the worlds of home and work, society and church, relationships and independence, the inner world and the outer world. This book affirms that women's paths, which are multiple and varied, have for too long been hidden or deemed inconsequential.

Walking in Two Worlds was an experience before it became a book. The contributors have all been presenters in the Theological Insights program at The College of St. Catherine, St. Paul, Minnesota. Over the past five years, they, together with other speakers and listeners, have gathered in Friday morning sessions to reflect on their spiritual paths, seeking answers to their questions about God or figuring out what questions to ask. Some, feeling increasingly invisible and lonely in a predominantly male church, looked for ways to connect with other women who felt the same. They never dreamed they would stand before a large audience and share intimate details of their life stories, let alone see those details appear in print. Women presenters who were more experienced in public or academic life had other wisdom to share: stories from research that uncovered important information buried in specialized texts or exciting new trends not yet common knowledge.

Realizing that minimal records of women's experience exist in historical tradition, the organizers of the Theological Insights program saw an opportunity to correct this lack. Although theological reflection seems to belong solely to the scholar, it, in fact, belongs to all. We cannot let this wisdom slip away or become invisible.

The individual contributors, like their audiences, represent most of the major Christian denominations and the Jewish faith, but they are in various stages of commitment—some deeply satisfied with their church, others troubled. Some have left formal worship for a while to sort things out. Ranging in age from thirty to seventy, these women represent a variety of occupations. Included among them are homemakers, church and community volunteers, teachers, students, pastoral workers and spiritual directors, and writers.

With this book we hope to extend Theological Insights beyond the gathering of women who came to The College of St. Catherine on certain Friday mornings. We hope that many read *Walking in Two Worlds* and that some may decide to write and speak for themselves.

The first Theological Insights series, offered in the autumn of 1987, was patterned after a program coordinated by Elizabeth Dodson Gray at Harvard Divinity School. As in the Harvard program, each session had two speakers focusing on a theme or issue. One speaker used her own experience to present a situation or raise a question about her relationship with God, with others, and with herself; the other brought an academic focus. Both gave perspectives on being women of vision today. The rich mix of material selected from the first five years of the Theological Insights program forms the text of this book and is organized in a similar way.

The aim of the Theological Insights series and this book is to turn raw experience into reflection and to turn reflection into empowerment. This empowerment has affected the lives of individual contributors in singular ways. One speaker, pleased with her ability to share with the audience, discovered the courage to translate that newfound confidence into other areas of her life. She went white-water rafting, and later began down-hill skiing because, as she said, "If I could do that (speak about my experiences), I could do anything!"

The speakers' empowerment transferred to many who, through listening, found their own voices and their own messages. "This program has reinforced some of my own beliefs," remarked one participant. "It has given me additional courage to return to school and has added clarity to some abuse issues at work. This courage is moving me to make a job change, a major decision."

One of the more difficult tasks in editing this book has been the selection of manuscripts. Not all presenters were able to submit manuscripts because they had used material from their own copyrighted works or because time constraints prevented them from preparing a written text. Topics have been revisited, nuanced, and further developed over the five years; to include all available manuscripts would have been repetitious. Space became the major limitation on the number of presentations to be included.

We thank The College of St. Catherine for sponsoring the Theological Insights program through its Office of Continuing Education and the Department of Theology. We appreciate the encouragement of Michael Murphy, Academic Dean at the time of the program's inception, and the assistance of the Director of Continuing Education, Kathryn Adam, and staff members throughout the five years—Lisa Brienzo, Janet Ditmanson, Judith Alley, and Bridget Reynolds. We thank Janice Weniger, secretary of the Theology Department, for her typing assistance.

We are grateful for the cooperation, encouragement, and enthusiasm of Elizabeth Dodson Gray and her husband, David Dodson Gray, who shared their experiences so that this program might become a reality in the Midwest. The Theological Insights core committee focused the themes and topics generated by the participants in the brainstorming that followed each session and guided the program from the beginning. That committee included Corinne Cavanagh, Mary Pinney Erickson, Karen Fitzpatrick, Rae Gardner, Kathy Hanousek, Louise Hiniker, Sharon Horgan, Linda Hutchinson, Theresa King, Betty Kling, Cheryl Maloney, Sarah Maney, Cathy Manion-Norgard, Mary Kaye Medinger, Maureen Neerland, Margaret Nelson, Bea Palmer, and Jane Soshnik.

Kay Vander Vort served as coordinator of the Theological Insights program and Joan Timmerman as theology faculty advisor. Eleanor Lincoln, professor of English, edited the manuscripts and helped shape the book.

Walking in Two Worlds is a tribute to the participants in the series, many of whom say that this group of women (and a few men) has become their primary spiritual community. They come from the metropolitan area of Minneapolis and St. Paul as well as from small towns within one hundred miles or more of the Twin Cities. Evaluative comments have been resoundingly positive:

"Listening to women telling their stories with courage has helped me to be faithful to my own life."
"I am blessed to know I have a community! My work at a law firm

pays the mortgage; my worship at church is merely shallow. I am desperate for *meaningful* spiritual searches and long to share the road with others."

"I am thrilled at the amount of wisdom women share. I have been both affirmed and empowered."

These are the walkers in two worlds, who recognize the truth in both. They are the ones who make it rewarding for the presenters so that it has been possible to evoke the best from the best without need for honoraria or stipends. To participate in this kind of community, committed to honoring women's experience of spirituality, has been its own reward.

Eleanor Lincoln
Joan H. Timmerman
Kay Vander Vort

May 1, 1992

Walking in Two Worlds
WOMEN'S SPIRITUAL PATHS

1.

In the Beginning: Reflections on Genesis

*We have a power in walking in two worlds, because
each one critiques the other. I think sometimes we
underestimate the power of that . . . to let the Bible and
the political structure critique each other.*
CORINNE CAVANAGH
Theological Insights, October 20, 1989

A Story of Healing

Marilyn J. Beckstrom

We shall not cease from exploration
And the end of all our exploring
Will be to arrive where we started
And know the place for the first time.

T.S. Eliot[1]

My work is pastoral counseling. Every day I sit with people who bring me their stories. Each person comes with pain and with hope. In the telling and the listening, in the interpreting and the re-interpreting, we make meaning. We reweave the tapestry of a life. I bring to this ministry my training and my own story. I also bring the Story with a capital "S," the Gospel Story, and the particular stories of the Hebrew and Christian scriptures and the tradition of the church. They are healing for those to whom I minister and healing for me.

But it has been a long journey to find healing. Some of the Biblical stories that I learned very early hurt more than they healed. But these stories are part of what has shaped me. I can reclaim these stories now, but only after long exploration. For many years they were part of a message in which I denied my own story, my own experience—both to myself and to others.

What was it like to be me at age ten or eleven? Come with me to the family farm in southwest Minnesota on a Sunday morning. I would have gone to Sunday School, having completed my Sunday School lesson Saturday night, and then to worship service with my mother, father, two older sisters, and younger brother. I would have come home to eat a large meat-and-potatoes dinner with pie for dessert. With my sister, I would have washed the dishes.

On Sunday afternoons other families, usually church families, came for coffee, or we went to their homes. If we stayed home, I might read or roam the farm. I was secure in knowing that I could daydream almost as long as I liked. No one could find me unless I chose to answer the calls.

After evening chores and supper we would go to church again for the evening Gospel service, an evangelistic service with lots of singing, a sermon about sin, and an altar call. I cannot sing that old hymn, "Just As I Am," without remembering Sunday nights in the rural church where I grew up.

I went to Sunday School every single Sunday. Everyone in the family collected rewards for perfect attendance—a round pin for the first year, a wreath encircling it for the second, and a small bar for each subsequent year. I had a pin several inches long that I wore every Sunday on my coat. Even on our rare vacations my mother would insist that we find a church so that the children would not miss Sunday School.

My world, as well as my Sunday, was defined by church. The particular kind of conservative protestantism of the church of my childhood demanded a withdrawal from the rest of the world creating a narrow world with strong boundaries and clear expectations for belief and behavior. There were more "don'ts" than "dos." I learned that the created world is not good, contrary to what the first creation story tells us God said. In H. Richard Niebuhr's categories from *Christ in Culture*, the church in which I grew up would be classified as Christ against culture.[2]

For many years, the church ten miles away from our farm was the core of my family's life and, therefore, my life. I learned that the people who went to our church were good and safe and were my community, not the family across the road or the children with whom I went to school in the small town three miles away. Until I was fourteen years old and went to a high school in a town of ten thousand, my closest friends were children from church. From age fourteen on, I lived in three different worlds and had three groups of friends—church friends, farm friends (the neighbor kids who were in 4-H club), and school friends from town. I was never able to integrate the three groups. I moved back and forth among them, never feeling as though I quite fit anywhere.

With this personal story as context, let us take a look at what I learned from the creation stories. As a child I learned only one creation story—the one in Genesis 2 where the female is created out of the rib of the male. The other story in Genesis 1 where God affirms that creation is good and male and female are created at the same time must have been suppressed. In the tradition in which I grew up, there could not possibly be two stories, unless they were exactly the same. Truth needed to be one and literal. It would have taken all sorts of mental gymnastics to try to reconcile the two stories.

The story I learned tells of the disobedience of Adam and Eve and their expulsion from the garden. Adam and Eve had done a very bad thing by eating the fruit. By eating the fruit, they had brought sin into the world, and now we were all sinners. It was not difficult for me to believe that I was born in sin. It was some explanation for how bad I often felt about myself. Punishment followed sin. After Adam and Eve were thrown out of paradise, they had to work hard. I knew about hard work on the farm. And childbirth would be painful. I heard the stories of my mother and her women friends.

What I learned from the creation story can be summarized in the following statements: I am, in my essence, bad. I am dependent on men. I am to blame. These themes ran through my life.

I learned that Eve was responsible for tempting Adam. If it hadn't been for Eve, we would probably all still be in paradise. Being born female increased my badness. Preference for males was in the story and was reinforced in my family. I was the third daughter, born months after my parents moved to Minnesota from Nebraska to risk all in buying a farm. My parents had been married ten years by the time I was born. They needed a son to continue farming.

I was supposed to have been David Gustaf. (Gustaf is my father's first name.) My parents gave that name to my brother who was born seven years later. I heard the stories about how my parents did not have a name picked out for me, because they were expecting a boy. I do not think that those stories were meant to hurt me, but they did.

I was aware early that I hated my brother. He was beautiful, smart and charming. My mother told everyone, "The girls just love him so." But I didn't. It was one more thing to feel guilty about. I could relate to the Cain and Abel story. Like Cain, I was just wrong. And my brother was right.

What was supposed to make me right was the one experience that everyone in my world absolutely had to have—the experience of "accepting Jesus Christ as your personal Savior." It was important to be saved as soon as one came to the age of accountability (six or seven). If a person were not saved, he or she would be damned.

I remember Sunday nights sitting in the back pew of the small country church and listening as adults stood to give testimonies about their conversion experiences. My uncle would talk on and on. I would be embarrassed and then feel guilty because I was embarrassed. Every Sunday night service included an altar call. Several times a year, visiting evangelists would come to town for a week or two to hold nightly meetings.

I was saved in vacation Bible school. Written in a small red Gideon New Testament are the words, "Marilyn Joyce accepted Jesus Christ as her Savior on June 6, 1947." Here it was, written down in blue ink. But I do not remember this experience. What I remember about daily vacation Bible school is eating lunches of fresh strawberries and ginger cookies under the spiraea bushes in the church yard and marching into the church every morning singing "Onward Christian Soldiers." Two boys led, carrying the Christian and United States flags. I remember sword drills—contests to see who could find a passage of scripture most quickly. I usually won. I remember many things about daily vacation Bible school. But I do not remember being saved.

And as I grew older, I began to doubt that I ever had been saved. I thought, "How could I be saved if I could not even remember it happening?" Maybe I had pretended to be saved? Shameful. My feelings of being bad intensified.

The doubt developed into fear. I had gone to all those evangelistic meetings and seen those elaborately colored charts of the End Times and the Second Coming with their chronologies of what was going to happen. I heard about the rapture, premillenialism, and postmillenialism.

My childhood fear formed its fullest expression in an experience I had when I was about eleven years old. On a gray November afternoon I had come home to the farm on the school bus. No one else was home. In the deepening twilight, waiting for my family to return, I began to imagine that the Second Coming—the rapture—had happened. Jesus had returned to earth and had taken all the saved folks with him, leaving all the unsaved behind. I had been left behind. The lights at other farms were little comfort. I did not know whether the neighbors were really saved. I remembered the Bible story: two will be grinding at the mill, one will be taken and the other left behind. I was certain that I had been left. My parents did come home, finally. But not until I had been jerked between hope and despair a half dozen times as car lights came down the road and did not turn into our driveway. My childhood imagination had been possessed, as James Fowler describes it in *Stages of Faith*.[3] I have often wondered why I did not express any of those fears to anyone. It simply did not occur to me.

As a young adolescent, I sat through those altar calls arguing with myself. I wanted to walk down the aisle because, somehow, that act might finally make me saved. Yet, I was overwhelmed by shame at the thought of exposing myself. A few years later I felt angry about the expectations that I should give my heart and life to Jesus. I wanted my own life. Then, in reaction, I felt guilty. Only as an adult did I realize that I had been trying as a young child to give up a self I did not yet have. By then I had some awareness that such demands of my church were inappropriate at best and damaging at worst.

I would not have you believe that my childhood was all gray fear and isolating shame. Like all human beings, I created my character armor. I needed to survive. A friend of mine asked me recently as we ate dinner whether I ate fast because there was not enough food on the table in my childhood. I replied that there always had been plenty of food. When I mentioned her observation to my brother, he said without a pause, "You wanted to read your book." Reading and creating imaginary worlds with my paper dolls or doll house furniture were my escapes, my defenses. They were also my hopes and plans for my future. They were how I hung on to the core that was Marilyn.

Another defense was achievement. I became a competent young woman. Doing well brought affirmation and an intermittent sense of well-being. I participated in church, school, and community activities. I loved to sing duets with my sister and solos for Sunday evening church services. We all took piano lessons. I sang in choir and played the bass clarinet in the band in high school. I belonged to 4-H and learned to do all those things that make a good wife—and a virtuous woman—cooking, baking bread, canning, sewing. My sisters and I did not raise pigs or calves. Those were things that boys did. My first sewing project at age eight was a blue and white sundress made from cloth feedsacks. Every summer until I was seventeen my sister and I sewed dresses to take to the county and state fairs. We were very accomplished girls, ready to marry.

I presented to the world around me a competent person. But I could not feel it. I recall one of the few intimate conversations I had with my best friend as a teenager. I told her that I never felt good enough. She said that this didn't make sense, pointing out my accomplishments. I insisted that it did not make any difference. I no longer needed the church to tell me I was unacceptable. I had absorbed the message.

I also learned from the creation story to be dependent on men. Who my father was and who my husband would be were critically important. The story of Eve, formed from the rib of Adam, shaped how I and those around me thought and felt. My models were mostly farming families. Men and women had defined roles, although women could step out of theirs—to drive the tractor, milk, or chop off chicken heads—as long as it was seen as helping men. Women dropped everything, literally, to run and help men. In church I saw that men were pastors, deacons, trustees—in leadership roles. Women could sing, play the piano, teach small children in Sunday School, serve lunch after funerals, bake the bread for communion and wash the little glasses afterwards.

The two fantasies I created illustrate my hopes and my inner conflict. I played them out with paper dolls under the dining room buffet. In Fantasy A, I went off to college. After college I would do something important and wonderful. In Fantasy B, Prince Charming fell in love with me and carried me off to live happily ever after.

My dependence on males was much deeper than I would know for a very long time. Part of me struggled against it and another part of me went along with it gladly. I went steady with a nice young man in high school. I wore his ring on a chain around my neck. I went to all the baseball, basketball, and football games with other girls to watch him play. I waited for him after games. The twelve-year-old Marilyn who had played second base on the softball team for Bigelow Elementary School, the only girl with eight boys, had disappeared. I was content to sit in the bleachers and cheer him on, until I was a senior. Then that other fantasy grew stronger—of going to college. I began to plan going two hundred miles away to St. Paul to the church-affiliated college where our pastor's daughter was a student. My father was against the plan. Girls just got married anyway. I convinced my mother, and she convinced my father, just as she had done so many other times. Just as Eve convinced Adam, I guess. I left home.

After two years of college, I stopped fully participating in the church of my childhood. But its influences did not leave me. It had shaped me more than I knew. Sometimes in those years I believed I had deserted God. Sometimes I felt that God had deserted me. Other times I did not think about God. I spent time walking and thinking, more time sitting in silence in Catholic churches. I did not know how to find a community of faith.

My senior year I was depressed, although I never named it then. I was feeling my own emptiness and was waiting for Prince Charming. I was rescued by a scholarship for graduate school at the University of Minnesota where I began an M.A. in English literature. I lived with a group of women and enjoyed my studies. Then the Prince did come along. I fell in love with a man who was about to enter a seminary in Berkeley. During that next year I made a choice that many women make. I chose to stop struggling with the fantasy of doing something wonderful and important. I shaped my choices around him. I re-arranged my life and left graduate school after the M.A. to take a job teaching high school English. We married after his first year of seminary, and moved to San Francisco where I lived for the next fifteen years.

For the next several years, I taught school full-time, spent a year as a VISTA volunteer in rural Alaska, and had a baby, our daughter Maja. But these things took second place. I was preoccupied with making a bad marriage work. It had to work, for my very life depended on it. I did not need to make it work for physical survival or financial security since I had learned to take care of myself in those ways; it was my emotional and spiritual life that was at stake.

When we had been married about three years, we tried marriage counseling. Then the time came when there was nothing more to say to one another. We agreed to separate, and I sought a psychotherapist for myself. Her office, in a restored Victorian in San Francisco, was filled with hanging plants, books, and several comfortable chairs. It occurred to me on my first visit that only two chairs would ever be filled. It would be she and I, just the two of us. I could not try to get my husband to change. I could only change myself. I was both terrified and hopeful.

With hindsight, I realize that ours was a developmental divorce. Both of us were needy and had little to give. His withdrawing from me had as much to do with his need to separate from his family as it did with me. My holding on and pushing was about my need to make my relationship with my father work, about not letting myself be aban-doned. In being abandoned, all I would have left was myself, and that did not feel like much. I have come to understand that in marrying, I had attempted not only to work out my family issues but also to work out my salvation. I had expected that this one relationship with a man would satisfy my deepest longings. The failure of my marriage stirred the feelings of shame and worthlessness, sadness, and anger, feelings I had been somewhat successful at suppressing.

The pain of divorce was the pressure that cracked my tightly constructed defenses. Like a seed dormant until germination in the spring rain and warming ground, I let growth begin. Slowly I was able to let myself be vulnerable, to claim my feelings and needs. I realize I did not always have to work so hard at being the competent person. I could just be. I developed friendships that were supportive and constant. When I was about thirty, I remember reading Carl Rogers, on unconditional positive regard, and thinking, that is what I am receiving from my friends. I would not have called it grace then.

I had also begun to find greater fulfillment in my teaching. I became a department chair and began to create programs to raise consciousness about two forms of prejudice—racism in my school district and discrimination against gays and lesbians in the larger school system. I had been radicalized as a VISTA volunteer during a year in the Alaskan bush. But it took me several years to take action. In an interview for a San Francisco newspaper, I spoke out against a state proposition that would have made it possible for gays and lesbians, as well as people like myself who spoke out in support of gay rights, to be fired from their teaching jobs. I was beginning to find my own voice.

My teaching colleagues and friends became my community of faith. My spirituality focused on justice issues. Yet I continued to feel an inner emptiness. My search took me to the Unitarian Church and then to a class from a woman who was a Quaker and Jungian. She became my first spiritual director. From her I learned to claim my own experience. I learned, in the words of Oscar Wilde, that "to regret one's own experience is to arrest one's own development. To deny one's own experience is to put a lie into the lips of one's own life. It is no less than a denial of the soul."[4]

I journaled. I read. I paid attention to my own life, especially my dreams. I still have a yellowed card on my bulletin board quoting a woman patient of Jung's: "By keeping quiet, repressing nothing, remaining attentive, and by accepting reality—taking things as they are and not as I want them to be—by doing all this, unusual knowledge has come to me and unusual powers as well."[5] I was awakening to the deep spiritual longings that I had long suppressed. I found a community of faith, the Religious Society of Friends or Quakers. I was attracted to a life of common worship that nourished and motivated a life of service for peace and justice. I did not have to believe a certain dogma, and I did not have to have a certain experience. I felt that I was coming home.

Seven years after my divorce, I began seminary. As I stood on the campus of Pacific School of Religion in Berkeley that September day in 1979, I was aware that I stood only a few blocks from the seminary where my husband had been a student in 1965, the year I fell in love with him. I understood more fully the anger and disappointment I had felt when he quit seminary. I had been angry and disappointed for myself. I had needed him to live out that part of my life of which I was not yet aware. Beginning my studies at seminary was the outward expression of my taking back my projections. I could finally hear the call myself.

My third childhood learning from the creation story was about blame and responsibility. I had learned that Eve was to blame for Adam's eating the fruit. Eve was responsible for Adam's choice. I had also learned to be responsible for the other person's feelings, behavior, and well-being. I had learned to be over responsible for others and under responsible for myself. When I was first married, I brought home the paycheck, did the housework, the childcare, and made my husband's lunch for him to take to graduate school. He did not have to demand it. I grew up believing that was what I was supposed to do. I left working in the public schools after thirteen years, saying only half facetiously that I could not bear the burden of the illiteracy of the students in that California suburb any longer.

In leaving teaching and beginning seminary I was taking fuller responsibility for myself. I made a series of decisions in the next several years; to go to seminary, to spend several months at Pendle Hill (a Quaker community), to move to Minnesota to live and work at a retreat center, and to do clinical training. I struggled to become responsible for myself and for others, especially my daughter. Moving to Minnesota meant that she would have to leave her friends and see her father less frequently. It was a difficult decision.

Women are given the responsibility for relationships. We judge ourselves in terms of our ability to care. It is difficult for me to include myself in the circle of those for whom I care, but when I do not consciously include myself, I try to get my needs met indirectly. And, I become manipulative, exhausted, and resentful.

It is still difficult for me to take responsibility for myself and allow the other person to be responsible for herself/himself. The shift began that day I sat in the therapist's office realizing that I could work to change only myself. It is a grace-filled process that continues. Healing has happened as I have learned from other women, friends and colleagues, my sisters and sister-in-law, my daughter, and my women's group, and many men as well. There are places of healing also: Pendle Hill, Arc Retreat Community, United Theological Seminary of the Twin Cities where theologizing out of my own experience was not only accepted but expected, the pastoral counseling centers where I trained.

Out of my own continued healing has come my ministry of pastoral counseling. In the spiral of my journey, I have come home to the church—to the place where I started. I can stand now at its center, celebrating and affirming, and at its edges, challenging and questioning. And, I have come home to myself. ". . . And the end of all our exploring / will be to arrive where we started / and know the place for the first time."[6] Eliot's words point to what has been happening and what continues to happen to me: the dynamic, dialogical process of co-creation that is my life.

I can come round again to the creation stories as well. I know them differently now and can reclaim much of them. I now hear more in them than the message that I am bad, dependent on men, and to blame.

I can reclaim the first creation story I could not hear as a child. This litany of creation repeats the phrase again and again, "And God saw that it was good." It has taken me a long time to believe that God celebrates the created world as good. It has taken even longer to believe it about myself.

I also reclaim the second Genesis story with its account of disobedience and expulsion from the garden. The first story tells us that the created world is good. The second tells us that humans make choices that separate us from God. Juxtaposed, these two stories tell me what it is to be human. I need both stories. This affirmation of the goodness of creation allows me to look at my capacity to choose evil. Darkness is indeed present in me, although it is not always the darkness that others have named. When I experience my worth to God, then I am able to own my darkness and confess my disobedience. And in claiming all I am, I move toward wholeness and holiness.

I am glad that there are two creation stories (just as I am glad that there are four Gospels). I infer affirmation of plurality and diversity from the very existence of more than one story. Two stories out of two traditions suggest to me that there is not just one right story. And not just one right experience of God. Two stories present the necessity of questioning and the possibility of growing.

If there is more than one story of creation, then there can be more than one way to be human. Then my unique experience can also be affirmed. My story does not have to match the single right story. "No two created beings are exactly alike, and their individuality is no imperfection. . . . For me to be a saint means to be myself."[7]

The creation stories are about what it means to be human. I am part of a good creation, and I have the capacity to choose. If I wanted to guarantee staying in the garden, I could never risk making a choice. I cannot stay in the garden and grow. Making choices means risk and pain and joy. Taking responsibility for myself means hard work. My co-creating my own identity in God is "a labor that requires sacrifice and anguish, risk and many tears."[8] It is paradoxically both a work and a gift of grace.

It takes courage to make choices. But I imagine that I can hear God saying now and then, as I risk, "It is good. It is very good."

1. T. S. Eliot, "Little Gidding," in *Four Quartets* (San Diego: Harcourt, Brace, Jovanovich, 1943), 59.

2. Richard H. Niebuhr, *Christ and Culture* (New York: Harper and Brothers, 1951), 45-82.

3. James W. Fowler, *Stages of Faith* (San Francisco: Harper and Row, 1981), 134.

4. Oscar Wilde, "De Profondis," in *The Soul of Man and Prison Writings* (Oxford: Oxford University Press, 1990), 100.

5. Carl G. Jung, "Alchemical Studies," in *The Choice Is Always Ours*, eds. Dorothy Berkeley Phillips, Elizabeth Bowden Howes and Lucille M. Nixon (Wheaton, IL: Re-Quest Books, 1948), 127.

6. Eliot, 59.

7. Thomas Merton, *New Seeds of Contemplation* (New York: New Directions, 1961), 29-31.

8. Ibid., 32.

Created for Freedom

Catherine Litecky

Elaine Pagels, in the introduction to her book, *Adam, Eve, and the Serpent,* writes that, after considerable research, she came to the conclusion that for the first four hundred years of the common era, Christians regarded freedom as the primary message of the creation myths recounted in the first three chapters of Genesis. That freedom, she says, was found in many forms, including "free will, freedom from demonic powers, freedom from social and sexual obligations, freedom from tyrannical government and from fate."[1]

That the creation myths could be a source of freedom for Christians in that early, vibrant period of the church comes as a surprise to many of us for whom the primary message of the story of creation has come to be an oppressive domination of men over women and of humans over the earth. In a recent newspaper article, entitled "A Feminist Reading of the Bible Shows Another Face of Eve," Pamela Milne, associate professor at the University of Windsor, points out that "the story of Eve has had a more profound negative impact on women throughout history than any other biblical story," having been interpreted for at least 2,000 years, "in patriarchal and even misogynist ways by male biblical scholars and theologians."[2]

It is certainly true in the United States that the inequality of the sexes stems in large part from the interpretation of the woman as subordinate and inferior to Adam and as the cause of evil in the world.

These interpretations were held by the Puritan ministers whose teach ings dominated the religious culture of the American colonies and pro foundly influenced the curriculum of the public schools and seminarie well into the twentieth century. Other theologians from the variou religious traditions also supported this interpretation throughout mucl of American religious history. Unfortunately, some continue to d so.

Are the creation stories, then, a clarion call to freedom, or ar they, as so many biblical fundamentalists have interpreted the stories a warrant for the oppression of women? I would like to consider som of the theological implications of the creation stories as they have bee interpreted and look at some possibilities for reinterpreting the myth of creation into a new theology of creation, one that leads to liberation

The authors of the creation stories were persons of faith who knev the God of liberation through the Exodus event before they knew th God of creation. Some time after the establishment of the Davidi kingdom (most likely in the court of Solomon about 950 B.C.), an imag inative scribe, a writer who has come to be called the Yahwist, wrot the story of creation found in Genesis 2. This writer called God "Yah weh" and described God in anthropomorphic terms. God, speakin; and acting like a human person, is imaged as a potter taking clay shaping it, and breathing into that form the breath of God.

In the other story found in Genesis 1, creation is described b theologian Monika Hellwig, as ". . . a series of seven tableaux in whic an ordered, harmonious, habitable universe is brought forth out o apparent chaos by God's command."[3] The writer or writers of thi account, called the Priestly source, wrote for the Jews who were exile in Babylon. All the exterior forms of their religion, like the great templ in Jerusalem in which they had put so much trust, had been destroyec In this critical period of near despair of the spiritual sons and daughter of Moses and David, the priests became the leaders of the people be cause they had no king. The task of the Genesis 1 writers, along wit that of the prophets of the exile, Jeremiah and Ezechiel, was to giv the people hope that the God who rescued their ancestors from Egyp would also liberate them. This all-powerful God, whose word coul accomplish what it willed, brought creation into existence.

The Priestly authors borrowed the framework for their story o creation from the Babylonian myth of creation known as the *Enum Elish*. In this myth, based on the world view or cosmogony held at tha time by all peoples in the ancient Middle East, the first three days wer days of separation when light was separated from dark, earth fror ky, and earth from water. Following this, God filled the world with plants, animals, fish, and greater and lesser lights. When all the world's furnishings were in place finally on the sixth day, "God created man in his image; in the divine image God created him; male and female God created them" (Genesis 1:27).

In this key sentence, the Priestly authors depart drastically from the pagan ideas found in *Enuma Elish*. The Babylonian myth gave as the principal reason for the creation of humans the desire of the gods and goddesses for slaves who would do their menial work. The Creator God of Genesis did not want or need slaves. Rather, the God of the Israelites wished to share divinity with humanity by creating humans in God's image. And this God is so pleased with the results of creation that God says it was "very good." It is important to note that in this story of creation, male and female are created simultaneously. The woman is not created after or from Adam.

The Priestly writers wanted to show the transcendence of God and God's wisdom, goodness, and power through which all things are made and on which they depend for their continuing existence. Like these authors, the psalmist who wrote Psalm 104, a song in praise of creation that follows the order of creation described in both the *Enuma Elish* and Genesis 1, says, "If you take away their breath, they perish and return to their dust" (Psalm 104:29).

The writers of the creation stories were not trying to give a scientific or philosophical explanation of how the world came into being or of how human beings came into existence. They were not asking or answering "how" questions; rather, they were attempting to deal with the meaning of human existence. They asked questions such as: "Why do we exist?" "What is the meaning of our lives?" "What do we do with all the other forms of creation?" "What does it mean to be created in the image of God?"

These creation stories tell us, in the language of poetry, that life is a gift, that we are contingent beings, that we are to be caretakers of the earth, and that we are given freedom, but freedom with boundaries. And just as God rested on the seventh day, we human beings are to rest and to contemplate so that we will keep alive in our minds and hearts the truth that we are indeed made in the image of God and are dependent on God for our continuing existence.[4]

Until recently, little attention has been paid to this theology of the first story of creation. Rather, the emphasis has been placed on the stories found in chapters two and three of Genesis, on the creation of Eve from Adam's rib and on the role of Eve in the story of the origin of evil. Because, in the Yahwist version, Eve was created after Adam and from his rib, she was regarded as subordinate and inferior to him. For her role in the sin story, she and all other women have been regarded as somehow weak and seductive.

These traditional interpretations of Genesis 2 and 3 became so deeply rooted that challenging them was difficult. One such intrepid challenger, however, was Elizabeth Cady Stanton, who in 1895 published *The Woman's Bible*, in which she reinterpreted the story of Eve. She wrote, "It is amazing that any set of men ever claimed that the dogma of the inferiority of woman is here set forth. The conduct of Eve from the beginning to the end is so superior to that of Adam." Stanton's efforts at biblical scholarship, like her efforts to obtain the vote for women in her lifetime, were, for the most part, ignored. However, *The Woman's Bible* has been reissued and more attention is now being given to Elizabeth Cady Stanton, especially by feminists.[6]

With the rise of feminist theology in the 1960s and the careful research of respected biblical scholars like Phyllis Trible of Union Theological Seminary, the creation stories are now beginning to be reinterpreted. According to Trible, "The problem with the Eve story is not the text itself, but the centuries of accrued sexist context that had grown up around it."[7]

Trible says, for example, that in the second story of creation patriarchal interpreters claim that man is superior because he is created first. However, in the story found in Genesis 1, animals are created before humans. Are humans, therefore, inferior to animals because the animals are created first? Or to take a different approach, if humans are the pinnacle of creation in Genesis 1, what is to prevent our saying that Eve is the crowning achievement in Genesis 2? After the serpent's temptation, Eve is blamed for being weak and gullible. The text doesn't say why the serpent spoke to the woman first. Trible says it is just as possible to speculate that the serpent spoke to Eve because she was the more intelligent of the two or because she had a better understanding of the command from God. Feminist biblical scholars generally hold with Phyllis Trible that the story of Eve can be reinterpreted to be a strong, positive message of sexual equality.[8]

Biblical scholar Karl Hermann Schelkle, in discussing creation and sin in his book, *The Spirit and the Bride: Women in the Bible* agrees that it is very questionable that Genesis 3 was intended to portray woman as yielding easily to temptation and causing the fall of man, even though many exegetes have interpreted the story in this way.[9]

Interestingly, this story of sin and punishment in Genesis 3 seems to have been forgotten for centuries in Israel until the intertestamental period. Initially the sin of Adam was the focus of attention, but gradually more and more emphasis was placed on Eve.[10] The author of Sirach 25:24 wrote, "From a woman, sin had its beginning and because of her, we all die." Some of the apocryphal literature of the intertestamental period put further blame on Eve, so much so that eventually Eve became the principle of all evil, according to Philo.[11]

We need to be aware, then, that the creation stories in Genesis are not to be taken literally or regarded as scientific history. They reflect a historical faith in the God who called the Israelites from slavery to freedom. Not only could God bring them to freedom, this God could call the whole world into being. The Priestly account teaches that the world exists for human beings, who are created in the image of God. The biblical authors tell us that evil exists and that inequality of the sexes is a result of sin; however, they do not say that Eve, the mother of the living, is the principle of evil.

Far from associating woman with evil, Teilhard de Chardin describes wisdom as "The Eternal Feminine" in a very beautiful, poetic essay:

> When the world was born, I came into being. Before the centuries were made, I issued from the hand of God—half-formed, yet destined to grow in beauty from age to age, the handmaid of his work. . . .
>
> Through me, all things have their movement and are made to work as one. I am the beauty running through the world, to make it associate in ordered groups: the ideal held up before the world to make it ascend. I am the essential Feminine."[12]

Teilhard de Chardin's experience as a paleontologist gave him unique insights into reading the biblical texts. For him, all life is process, and his lifelong search was for synthesis. He wrote ". . . evolution is not really creative as science at one time thought; rather it is the expression, in terms of our own experience, of creation as it unfolds in space and time."[13]

Recently, I came across a book, *The Sons of the Gods and the Daughters of Men: An Afro-Asiatic Interpretation of Genesis 1-11*, by a Nigerian exegete and philologist, Modupe Oduyoye. Like Teilhard, this writer brings special insights to the stories of creation based on his own sensitivity to the realm of the spirit and to linguistic understandings that we of the West do not possess. I was struck by some of his interpretations of the creation myths in Genesis. For example, in the

West African creation myths, the heavens and the earth were considered to be autonomous creative powers, male and female, who were created by sexual intercourse.[14] What the Yahwist author did in his story of creation was to demythologize a polytheistic interpretation of creation by making Yahweh not a parent but an artist able to create the human out of clay.

In Genesis 1 the Priestly writers also demythologized the pagan myth of creation by declaring that the sun and the moon and the stars were not gods as the pagans considered them to be but mere creatures of God. All created things came into being through God's command. The Priestly writers thus changed the metaphor of God from a plastic artist to one who commands because, according to Oduyoye, ". . . those who believe that God is an image-maker may be inclined themselves to make images . . ." and images were a constant danger to the monotheistic religion of the Jewish people during the time the Priestly authors wrote Genesis.[15]

We have seen that the Genesis stories of creation were written by monotheists who remembered that the God who liberated them from oppression was the God who created them for freedom. I would like now to look at the theology of creation from a liberation perspective.

Many of us may be familiar with the invocation, "Our help is in the name of the Lord who made heaven and earth" (Psalm 124:8) Dorothee Soelle, a German theologian, says that we can think of the word, "help," in this context, as a synonym for "liberation" or "freedom." We can say, therefore, "Our freedom is in the name of the God who created heaven and earth." Our question now is, "Why did God create the heaven and earth?"

In her book, *To Work and to Love: A Theology of Creation*, Soelle maintains that God created the world out of a desire for relatedness God is not a remote God, the Divine Architect or Clockmaker who put everything in place, set it in motion and, thereafter, was finished with creation, as many Deists believed. God who is Love (both noun and verb) needs humans. As Soelle says so movingly,

> Love needs the presence and involvement of another being; love cannot exist without the other. Self-sufficiency is a concept of the lonely and unrelated person. To conceive of creation in the framework of unrelatedness is to deprive creation of its most central element—love. . . . The concept of creation is rendered empty and meaningless if it is not out of love that God created the world.[16]

Aware of God's relationship to us, a new theology of creation see

he earth as holy. The traditional interpretation of the myths of creation
ias fostered the domination of the earth by humankind. Only in the
ast few years have we come to realize that ecological disasters may
ace us in the foreseeable future. Sadly, the prophet of these catas-
rophes, Rachel Carson, who published *Silent Spring* in 1962, was
reated with disdain by fellow scientists, who regarded her as an alarmist
ecause of her concern for the effects of pesticides on our food and
n our water.

We are coming to a much greater appreciation of caring for the
hings of this earth, to an awareness of the sacramental nature of
reation. That sacramental nature held so consciously by the Native
Americans is expressed in a speech given by the Squamish Chief Se-
ttle in Washington, D.C., in 1854 to make the transferral of ancestral
ndian lands to the federal government. We can learn much about rev-
rence for creation from him:

> How can you buy or sell the sky, the warmth of the land? The idea
> is strange to us . . .

> Every part of this earth is sacred to my people. Every shining pine
> needle, every sandy shore, every mist in the dark woods, every
> clearing and humming insect is holy in the memory and experience
> of my people. . . .[17]

How do we share the earth with God? How do we become persons
vho choose life and freedom instead of death and oppression? The
itle of Dorothee Soelle's book, I think, supplies the answer—in our
ibility to *work* and *love*. Sigmund Freud was asked once how he would
characterize a sane person, and he described the person who had the
ibility to work and to love. We participate in creation then through
oving and working, through being alive and sensitive to that which
vill be freeing for ourselves and others.

For Christians in those first centuries, to which I alluded earlier,
conversion was not so much to knowledge of the faith but to a new way
of life that liberated the early Christians from the deadness of the sec-
ilar culture in which they lived.[18]

How can we continue to choose life or to choose it more fully and
reely? If it is through love and work that we collaborate with God in
reation, probably the first way that comes to mind for many people
s the mother-child relationship, a love expressed in the physical caring
hat certainly includes spiritual and psychological components. That
ame inter-relationship, according to Carol Ochs in her book, *Women
ind Spirituality*, ". . . holds for the love between lovers, siblings, friends,

colleagues and, perhaps, for the love of all being (what Albert Schweitzer calls 'reverence for life')."[19] How we treat all objects, animate as well as inanimate, indicates our relationships to those objects. Love that is nonpossessive and nonmanipulative belongs to the realm of freedom and creativity.[20]

A liberating theology of creation must also include the human capacity to perceive beauty. The Hebrew word for "good," used repeatedly in Genesis 1, can be translated as "beautiful." Thus God could have said at the completion of creation, "It is all very beautiful." Artists who create beauty in all its forms are, in a very real sense, co-creators with God.

In an ideal world, the relationship between our love and our work would be obvious, but, for many people in the real world, work can be alienating and dehumanizing. The meaning of work, however, is not to be found in the work itself but in the relationship of the work to the worker. Ochs gives the example of a person who cleans cesspools but enjoys his work because he works out-of-doors, helping to keep the natural world clean.[21] We all could mention people doing what we might consider distasteful or boring jobs, people who bring a luminous quality to their work because of the motivation of their lives. Dorothee Soelle offers a vision of work that gives priority to self-expression, social relatedness, and reconciliation with nature. Work involving these priorities would indeed be liberating and creative.

A new creation theology, like all good theologies, must be based on human experience and longing. May all of us in the everyday experiences of our lives come to know as fully as possible that we are indeed created for freedom.

1. Elaine Pagels, *Adam, Eve, and the Serpent* (New York: Random House, 1988), xxv.

2. Pamela Milne, "A Feminist Reading of the Bible Shows Another Face of Eve," *The Minneapolis Star Tribune*, 26 March 1989, 25A.

3. Monika Hellwig, *Understanding Catholicism* (New York: Paulist Press, 1981), 31.

4. Ibid., 29-32.

5. As quoted in Milne, 24A.

6. Elizabeth Cady Stanton, *The Woman's Bible* (New York: Arno Press, 1972).

7. As quoted in Milne, 25A.

8. As quoted in Milne, 25A.

9. Karl Hermann Schelkle, *The Spirit and the Bride* (Collegeville, MN: The Liturgical Press, 1979), 9, 14.

10. Ibid., 21-22.

11. Ibid., 22.

12. Pierre Teilhard de Chardin, *The Prayer of the Universe* (New York: Harper and Row, 1968), 143.

13. Pierre Teilhard de Chardin, quoted in "Creation," *The New Dictionary of Theology* by Denis Carroll (Wilmington: Michael Glazier, Inc., 1987), 252.

14. Modupe Oduyoye, *The Sons of the Gods and the Daughters of Men: An Afro-Asiatic Interpretation of Genesis 1-11* (Maryknoll, NY: Orbis Books, 1984), 10.

15. Ibid., 11.

6. Dorothee Soelle and Shirley A. Cloyes, *To Work and to Love: A Theology of Creation* (Philadelphia: Fortress Press, 1984), 16.

7. As quoted in Soelle, 17.

8. Margaret R. Miles, "The Recovery of Asceticism," *Commonweal* (28 January 1983): 41.

9. Carol Ochs, *Women and Spirituality* (Totowa, NJ: Rowman and Allanheld, 1983), 15.

20. Ibid., 16.

21. Ibid., 14.

2.

Encountering Myth

*The time has come for a new genre of myth—
intimations are all around us, particularly in a room
full of women like this . . . we must move toward
myths that free us.*

MARCIA CASEY CUSHMORE
Theological Insights, April 15, 1989

Happily Ever After

Margaret Nelson

In marriage we commit ourselves to live out our lives with another person. How we do this is often shaped by the myths of our religious upbringing and the norms of society.

My marriage is a product of the 1950s, an era that saw a return to traditional family roles as the country emerged from the confusion of World War II. During the war years, some women had achieved a measure of independence. Like Rosie the Riveter, they had taken jobs in shipyards, factories, and railroad terminals. Some had joined the armed services themselves and even learned to fly airplanes. They found themselves not only capable of doing work traditionally done by men, but found that they could do such work well.

After the war years there was a concerted effort to return the situation to "normal"—when the men were strong and in charge of things and the women were perfect homemakers. It was time to lure Rosie the Riveter back to the kitchen.

The returning war heroes knew how to treat a lady. Chivalry was not yet dead. Not only did these heroes open car doors for a fair maiden and light her cigarettes, but they also rescued damsels in distress— particularly from the "distress" of being employed in dismal and dirty factories. There was a national reaction to the threat of women in the work force. Without those distressing jobs, women again needed protectors, knights in shining armor.

Without financial independence, women were forced to find other means of protection. The myth of the "good wife" was reborn with a vengeance. It was part and parcel of the postwar American myth of the "good life." Domestic bliss was promoted in popular books, films and magazines, and reinforced by traditional religious values. There was a new prosperity in the land and a rush back to the status quo.

The symbols of the good life were represented in popular culture as a house in the suburbs and a station wagon. TV gave the postwar family its best models in June Cleaver of "Leave It to Beaver" and Margaret Anderson of "Father Knows Best." These women were dutiful wives, patient and kind mothers, and always appeared doing their housework in modest dresses covered by aprons, while wearing low-heeled pumps and nylon stockings. These domestic heroines lived the myth that the "good wife" will live "happily ever after" in this world . . . and the next. All she had to do for her reward was to be chaste, prudent, frugal, faithful, keep a clean house, and be a perfect mother. This ideal was underscored by a proliferation of marriage manuals containing foolproof prescriptions for the perfect marriage.

It was assumed that every normal, healthy young woman would want to be married. A profusion of articles offered advice on how to catch a man and how to hang on to him once he was caught. It became important to be half of a couple. Everything was done in pairs. Not to be chosen for marriage was considered to be the "fate worse than death."

I was shaped by this culture that was bent on reestablishing the place of women in the home and by a church that had always understood the wife as secondary and submissive to the husband. This myth was painfully present in the nuptial blessing contained in the marriage rites of the Roman Catholic Church. This is the tale of my own marriage and my encounter with the myth—and of the discovery of my own truth.

The average young woman in the 1950s was married and had one child before her twentieth birthday. In 1954, I was twenty-one years old, the last of my high school crowd to walk down the aisle. I had convinced myself that I was indeed going to be an old maid, that I would not be chosen. In truth and honesty, I did not see that the good life would happen for me. I would not be part of the fairy tale.

So I prepared myself well for spinsterhood by entering nursing, a profession that would, I thought, provide for all my needs for the next forty or so years. Nursing also had the advantage of putting me in daily contact with doctors, understood then always to be rich, handsome and male. The remote possibility existed that one of them would sweep me off my feet. I secretly harbored the desire to be a wife and mother. Perhaps in the end I would be lucky enough to marry one of them.

Meanwhile, I was living a spinster life with five other nurses in a rented apartment. Hope was fading. I dated occasionally, but Dr. Right did not appear. Then I was asked on a blind date and, by the end of the evening, had fallen wildly, madly, passionately in love. I never looked at another man after I met Dick. Ours was a whirlwind court-ship—as romantic as could be—and I did truly feel like a fairy tale princess as my Prince Charming carried me off to live happily ever after.

As I knelt before God and in the presence of witnesses that sunny day in May 1954, to receive the nuptial blessing, I did not pay much attention to the words. What I was doing seemed right, and I was deeply in love. I finally would live out my true destiny in suburbia with a round of card parties and charitable bazaars, saved from the fate worse than death.

The nuptial blessing was more of a prescription for being a good wife than an actual blessing. As I reflect on that "blessing" now, I see how it linked me closely to Eve, the "sinful one" who led Adam astray. It was also calculated to keep me submissive to my husband, to be fruitful, hardworking, chaste, frugal, and a good and wise mother. At the time, the nuptial blessing in the *Daily Missal of the Mystical Body* seemed good to me and in keeping with the myth:

> **Let us pray.** O God, by your mighty power you have created all things out of nothing. You have arranged the forces of the world; you have made man in the image of God and have given him an inseparable helpmate in woman, even fashioning her body out of his flesh, and by this creative act teaching us the sinfulness of putting asunder that which you have formed out of a single substance. O God, you have sanctified the union of husband and wife by a sacrament so exalted that in the marriage bond you foreshadowed the union of Christ with his Church. O God, by your act of joining woman to man you have hallowed this union from the beginning with a blessing that was not lost either by the punishment for original sin or by the sentence of the flood. Look mercifully upon this handmaiden of yours who begs protection and strength of you as she is about to be joined in marriage. May it be for her a yoke of love and peace. Let her marriage, under Christ, be chaste and true; and in it may she follow the pattern of the holy women: may she be dear to her husband like Rachael, prudent like Rebecca, faithful

and long-lived like Sara. Let the Father of Lies work none of his evil deceits in her; but let her always be firm in faith and obedient to your commandments. May she be faithful to her husband, and flee illicit attachments; may she strengthen her own frailty by firm discipline; may she be sedate in her manner, recognized for her modesty, well founded in her knowledge of religious matters. May she be fruitful in offspring. May she be virtuous and innocent, and come to rest among the blessed in the kingdom of heaven. May they both see their children's children to the third and fourth generation, and may they reach an old age such as they desire. Through the same Jesus Christ, our Lord.[1]

The nuptial blessing said little to my husband, but that did not matter. I had already blessed him a hundred, a thousand times over. I had assigned him a role; church and society had also assigned him a role. To me he was rescuer and protector. To society he was bread-winner and provider.

I proceeded to become all those things a good wife was supposed to be: an impeccable housekeeper, imaginative cook, patient mother, and passionate bed partner. Like most young wives I idealized my role. I subscribed to *Good Housekeeping* and the *Ladies' Home Journal*, following their precepts religiously.

I became so closely bonded with the house in the suburbs—its contents and activities—that I merged with it. I was one of the good life symbols. My first inkling of this came with our first Christmas. My "big" gift from my Prince was a vacuum cleaner—and I was really thrilled! A deluxe model, it had all the attachments! Now I could keep the house even more immaculately clean, just as the ads promised!

I continued to read my magazines, which were by now no less than Holy Writ. They were full of household hints, recipes, child care articles, and advice on how to achieve simultaneous orgasm! This last was particularly important. I learned that if a couple failed to achieve simultaneous orgasm, it was the woman's fault. Women were warned to correct this failing or the men would be off to seek someone who would satisfy all their sexual appetites. I applied all this advice with uncritical determination.

I hung on to the good life for dear life. Burdensome as it was to be a good wife, I—was—going—to—be—one. I was not only going to be a good wife, I was going to be a *perfect* wife. And I was going to be the perfect mother as well. I had chosen this good life and I was determined to—Live—happily—ever—after.

But, gradually, reality set in. First of all, I finally admitted that I really didn't like housework, in spite of that wonderful vacuum cleaner. Intimate dinners for two and idyllic evenings before the fireplace gave way first to morning sickness and then to 2:00 A.M. feedings. Where had romance gone? Where was fulfillment in this life of colicky babies and dirty diapers? Where was the good life when the station wagon broke down between trips to the obstetrician and the pediatrician?

I had been led to believe—through my church, my magazine articles, and the television set—that the act of raising a child was as creative an effort as painting the ceiling of the Sistine Chapel. But my world had become incredibly narrow. I yearned to paint a picture, or write a short story, or even create an original recipe. I wanted to do something. I felt I needed to "steal" time for myself in order to participate in "other" creative enterprises, but, even then, the time was stolen back again by daily tasks. My creative juices were turned off by the reality of everyday life that wasn't so good.

The first time I encountered the truth behind the good wife myth, I was scrubbing the kitchen floor on my hands and knees. Miraculously, the word "scrub" floated into my mind. "Oh, yes. 'Scrub.' Remember? That's something you used to do when you worked in the operating room. And when you were finished, surgeons used to say, 'Thank you.' And you got a pay check every two weeks with your own name on it. There were rewards, and it was fun!"

I said to myself, "Wait a minute! Is *this* what I committed myself to? Where are the rewards?" Something began to stir within me, and I got up off my hands and knees, went to the phone, and made an appointment for a job interview with the director of nursing at the local hospital. I had come face to face with the myth of the good wife, and I found it distorted. I may have made a commitment to a marriage and to my husband, but I did not make a commitment to this definition of the good wife. Perhaps the good wife would indeed live happily ever after, but the definition imposed by society and perpetuated by the Church was false.

This was the beginning of my redemption. I began to work one day a week. I called it my therapy, far better than shopping for a new hat, the standard cure for housewife fatigue in those days. It was also the beginning of a new and more interesting relationship with my husband.

As I grew away from the myth of the perfect wife, my husband grew away from it too. As a couple, we truly began to understand the commitment we had made to each other on our wedding day. The commitment was not only to love one another, but to respect and encourage one another's growth, to give each other sacred space, to work together as equal partners, and to bide each other's time. From this understanding grew the legacy that we have given our children.

My first opportunity to bequeath that legacy came in May 1961. It was also the opportunity to confront the corollary myth of the perfect mother. I had become the mother of four boys, Mike, Jim, David and Dan. I was nursing the new baby, who was not yet a month old. It had just begun to rain, and diapers were hanging on the line. There were lots of diapers as my next oldest boy was only fourteen months old. As yet, no such thing as Pampers or Huggies had come on the market. My husband went out and started to bring in the diapers. Mike, our oldest son, then six, watched him from the kitchen door. His little hands were on his hips, and, from all the worldly wisdom and experience of almost a whole year in kindergarten, he said, "Why is Daddy out there doing women's work?"

Completely unbidden, without any conscious thought on my part, the first words out of my mouth were, "In this house there is no such thing as women's work!" It was, I believe, a graced moment.

From that time, we both made a conscious effort to prepare our sons to be equal partners in marriage. My husband had been sharing the household responsibilities, especially with child care, but now, he expanded his horizons and involved the boys in these tasks as well. Together they would dust the furniture and scrub out toilet bowls. At the same time, I began to assume more responsibility for bringing income into the home. Gradually our modeling of equal partnership had an impact on our sons, and I hope it will on their children as well.

Twenty-seven years later, Mike, now thirty-three, called to ask if I would show him how to make pasties! There is no real recipe for pasties. The technique has traditionally been handed down in my family from mother to daughter. As the mother of four sons, the best I had ever hoped for was to show a daughter-in-law how to make pasties some day. I had never dreamed I would hand on this tradition to a son! Mike brought his favorite paring knife and his five-year-old son Chris. The three of us spent a warm and wonderful Saturday afternoon cutting up vegetables and rolling out pastry. I beheld a beautiful sight—my son with flour on his jeans and a rolling pin in his hand instructing his son on the proper procedure for rolling out dough. It brought to mind that day in 1961 and the little tyke who was so concerned about women's work. I thought to myself, "We've come a long way, baby!"

There comes a time in marriage when we need to examine the practices and habits that have become our myths and reshape them to reflect our own growth and our own truth. I believe with all my heart that marriage is intended to be a growth-inducing state and therein lies its sacramentality. But within the marriage, we do remain individuals, each growing at different rates and different times. We do this from the truth that comes from within us, not by something our culture or our church imposes on us from without. In this way, through remythologizing, the myth becomes authentic again.

In my case, the truth came to me while I was scrubbing a floor— truth that I had gifts and abilities that cried out to be used in a, then, non-traditional way. My truth was to get up and act on that. My husband's truth was to support and encourage me. We each must seek our own truth and act on it or run the risk of being stuck in the metaphor and the myth. Being stuck is a failure to grow.

As I reflect on my story, I have concluded that if I were ever to receive another nuptial blessing, rather than sinful Eve, I would want to be linked more closely with Mary. She is the grace-filled one, the one who was complete and whole in her own person, the one who lived out her life with another, not in another or for another. I would want this second nuptial blessing to reflect the truth of equal partnership in marriage, respect for each other's wants as well as each other's needs, space to grow and be in our own truth, and, finally, the grace and the wisdom to offer this truth to the next generation. In this way, the "good wife" (and the "good husband") *will* live happily ever after.

1. Maryknoll Fathers with the collaboration of Charles J. Callan, O. P., eds., *Daily Missal of the Mystical Body* (New York: P. J. Kennedy and Sons, 1957), 644-45.

Once Upon a Time

Margaret L. Boettcher

Once upon a time, in this case, a rather recent time, I had a most amazing experience. On the surface, the details of my story may seem quite ordinary to most people—nothing, perhaps, to be considered earthshaking or volcanic in nature. But for me the experience was exactly that—earthshaking, riveting, a pivotal moment in time. On that fall day in 1988, I encountered myth—an experience that precipitated in me an explosion of feelings, questions, and concerns.

My daughter, a senior in high school at that time, and I, both musicians, had been asked to perform for the crowning of the high school king and queen at the Homecoming pageant. We were to accompany the entrance of the queen candidates into the gymnasium with a flute and piano piece. Early on the morning of the event, we rehearsed the ceremony with the participants. Later, during the actual event, I was seated in the midst of the percussion section. Behind me stood the tympani, snare drums, and xylophone, while the brass section curved away to my left.

The pageant began with the entrance of the candidates for king, accompanied by a thunderous arrangement of the theme from the movie *Superman*, a powerful score for band that employs full percussion and brass in an extravagant display of sound. Most of the candidates for king represented various athletic teams. Handsomely dressed in suits and ties, they were escorted into the gym by members

31

of the girls' dance line, which often performed at sports events, and by members of the cheerleading squad.

Because I had already sat through the rehearsal, I knew what came next, and, before the queen candidates even appeared at the door to the gym, I felt upset. I kept thinking, "I really don't like this! Something's wrong." My feelings were so intense that I no longer wanted to participate in the ceremony. Then the queen candidates arrived at the gym door, dressed in beautiful prom-style dresses, hair carefully arranged—some sprayed with glitter—many wearing sling-back shoes. *Their* accompanying music was the jazz piece—a soft, sweet melody for flute and keyboard played by my daughter and myself and an arrangement of the evocative Irish melody "Danny Boy," played by only the mellow woodwinds of the band. Young male athletes, representing various boys' sports and dressed like the king candidates in suits and ties, escorted these girls.

In spite of dealing with both negative and unexpected feelings, I completed my performance although, I did not enjoy the pageant. My reaction surprised me because I had witnessed many such events and never before had I felt that way. Now my mind whirled with questions: Why had we played the *Superman* theme with the full band and its spectacular sound for the boys, while we played the jazz piece for flute called "Sentimentale" and the melody "Danny Boy" for the girls? Why were the girls dressed like fairy-tale princesses and the boys like businessmen? Why did miniskirted cheerleaders and dance team members escort the male candidates while athletes dressed in suits ushered in the female candidates?

In the weeks following the pageant, I asked myself repeatedly why I had reacted so strongly to the Homecoming pageant. I decided that my reaction was related to the fact that the very week of the pageant, I was studying symbol, myth, and ritual at The College of St. Catherine in a course on sacramental theology. Also, just prior to the pageant, I had been energized by the first lecture in the fall 1988 "Theological Insights" series.

I remembered a comment made by a lecturer: "You recognize myth when it no longer works for you." I knew that I had experienced a powerful encounter of some kind at the high school ceremony, and something was definitely not working for me that day. Had I encountered myth? If so, what myth? What exactly was the deeper meaning I saw in the ritual? What values were being expressed?

The word "myth" as I use it means something other than the popular connotation of the word. Myth is a symbolic expression in narrative form of a deep truth. Ritual is symbolic language in the form of action. In order to better understand myth and ritual as symbolic expressions, I want to reflect first upon the meaning of symbol. According to Joseph Martos in *Doors to the Sacred*, "Symbols can be anything, gestures, actions, natural or man-made objects, spoken or written words, pictures or sounds, persons or places. What the symbol does is draw us out of the world of our everyday concerns and into a world which is associated with the symbol."[1] Symbols communicate meaning on a very deep level. Moreover, symbols possess many layers of meaning. By their very nature, they represent what cannot be fully expressed in words, that which has to do with the ineffable. Myth and ritual, then, are not about factual truth in the historical or scientific sense, but they are about truth as symbolically expressed.

Joseph Campbell, in his book, *The Power of Myth*, says that myth serves four functions. The first function is mystical: an invitation into the mystery of life, an invitation to realize what a wonder the universe is and what a wonder each person is, an invitation to experience awe before the mystery. The second function is cosmological; myth shows us the shape of the universe in such a way that the mystery comes through. In its third, or sociological, function, myth supports and validates a certain social order. And fourth, myth has a pedagogical function, showing us how to live a human life under any circumstances.[2]

Campbell's third function of myth, the sociological function that validates and supports a certain social order, is most relevant to my encounter with myth in the fall of 1988. Both myth and ritual represent social values and attitudes and reveal social tensions, struggles between good and evil, dark and light, male and female.

These definitions of myth and ritual are drawn primarily from a theological context. A question with which I struggled was "Can I apply these definitions to an experience that took place in a secular context, that is, the Homecoming pageant?" In *The Meaning of Ritual*, Leonel Mitchell says that Western society has largely rejected religious ritual but that Americans have many secular rituals that replace religious rituals. He gives as examples the Miss America Pageant, the Academy Awards, and pre-football game activities.[3] Mitchell affirms my belief that the Homecoming pageant functioned as a ritual with profound significance.

First, the pageant clearly fit the description of ritual: the ceremonial walk around the gym as the candidates were introduced; the speeches; the ceremonial music; the symbols of crown, robe, and scepter; and the special mode of dressing as exemplified by the fairy-tale dresses worn by the queen candidates, the business suits worn by the king candidates, and the cheerleaders' short miniskirts, which elicited catcalls and whistles from the male student body. What was the function of all this ritual? What deeper meaning and values were being conveyed? What norm represented the relationship between male and female in this pageant? What did the crown, robe, and scepter symbolize in a country without a monarchy?

I recalled a series of lectures on spirituality for liturgical ministers given by Father Kevin Seasoltz at St. John's University. He spoke of our competitive society, of our need to be number one, of our need to be at the top of the heap. In the process, we trample others to get there, and once we get there, we have to trample others to stay there. Seasoltz said that we live in a society where success is the ultimate reward. We must win; we must be the best. He also mentioned our adulation of the superstars in athletics, movies, and rock music.[4]

How do Seasoltz's comments about our competitive society apply to the Homecoming pageant? If ritual establishes or communicates the norm for social relationships, do the symbols of crown, robe, and scepter convey the meaning that these king and queen candidates are the ones in our society that really count? Because they are some of the cutest girls, the most handsome and macho boys, some of the most popular students, do they somehow have power and authority over the other more average students? What kind of expectations, what role models, does the Homecoming ritual establish? What norms? Are the norms helpful and encouraging, or are they depressing and discouraging for those who feel they can never measure up to the ideal of being number one?

And what about the costumes? The prom dresses and sling-back shoes for the girls and the suits and ties for the boys? If ritual is a language that speaks about social relationships and that reveals social tensions, what do these outfits say about male/female social relationships? These girls were competent, bright, athletic, and competitive. They had well-trained bodies, and had achieved successes in their own right. Many of them represented the best in girls' sports. So why did they dress like fairy-tale princesses? Why did only the boys get to march in to the theme of *Superman*? Why couldn't the girls—many of whom were strong, aggressive people—be ushered in to the theme of *Star Wars*? Why couldn't some boys march in to the emotionally evocative melody of "Danny Boy"? After all, they were capable of deep emotion and could be sensitive and caring individuals. In its language, the pageant used no symbolic narrative but it was symbolic action. A fairy-tale story seemed to lurk just under the surface with the princess figure waiting to be rescued by a knight in shining armor!

I am not going to summarize all the meanings of the Homecoming ritual. Symbol, by its nature, is multilayered in meaning and evokes many levels of response and interpretation. I can conclude, however, that I encountered in the Homecoming pageant a myth so powerful, so volcanic, so energizing that it formed a kind of bridge to the past, causing me to look back at other experiences in my life that had resulted in similar feelings. Applying the questions I had about myth, I recalled the ritual of another experience, which I call, "Encounter with a Sexy Broad."

A number of years ago, as a member of the governing board of an arts organization in my community, I was the primary mover behind a spring arts festival and concert. We wished to use an old historic building that was slated to be torn down. Over a period of four months, I negotiated with the owner of the building and the city council concerning a public use variance, adequate insurance in the event of a lawsuit, and the building of a ramp for the handicapped. After numerous meetings with the owner and the city council, both the ramp and the insurance were obtained and the public use variance was granted. After that, I personally solicited money from local banks and savings and loans institutions to promote the festival. Because we still lacked sufficient funds, it was agreed that I would represent the arts organization at a monthly meeting of a local group of business people to ask for contributions.

Envision this scene for a moment. Present at the meeting were more than forty men, all owners or managers of businesses. Present were two other women besides myself, the manager of a local store and the wife of the owner of the building in question. The meeting was held in the bar of a local restaurant. To my right were six men seated on a row of bar stools, most of them smoking. The man closest to me held a large cigar in his mouth.

After thoroughly explaining the lengthy process of negotiation already accomplished, I asked for a motion for financial support. The man seated closest to me, removed the cigar from his mouth, blew smoke in my direction, and looked at me with great intensity. He said, "Well, you know how these arts organization are—always asking for money. We all know how they operate! They send around a sexy broad to solicit our money. I'm opposed to this project, and my vote is no!" A gasp went around the room, and then silence filled the void left by his announcement.

I stood there, like Lot's wife who had been turned to a pillar of salt, unable to move, to say anything at all. I felt hot and angry, speechless in front of that group of people. I stood for what seemed an eternity. Then an older man spoke eloquently in support of my proposal and the arts in general, and the motion to grant us the money was voted in without dissent.

Until the fall of 1988, I had always remembered this incident as just a very unpleasant experience, one that I hoped never to repeat. However, in the light of my ponderings about the meaning of the Homecoming ritual and in the context of myth, I began to question: Was this an encounter with myth? Did this man's response have to do with images he had in his subconscious mind about women's roles?

If myth is a symbolic language that prescribes for human beings the mode of their being in the world and establishes the norm, then out of what myth, what archetype of women, did the cigar smoker draw his references? Certainly not mine. I obviously possessed an image of a woman who said, "Yes, I could be the mother of two small children, be a wife and care for a home, be a volunteer and function in an unpaid, semiprofessional capacity as an arts festival producer, and teach piano professionally." Though not always easily, I could and did walk in two worlds. But what myth defined this view of me?

As I struggled to situate my experiences in the context of myth, I read an article in *Outlook* that helped me understand the gentleman who had called me a "sexy broad." Author Lynn Schrafran wrote about gender bias in the United States Judicial System, saying that "many judges remain deeply attached to the concept of womanhood they believe to be symbolized by Mary—a woman for whom motherhood is the only appropriate goal, who remains at home participating in a limited range of activities in the domestic sphere; who does not assume positions of authority; whose chastity is unassailable."[5]

Schrafran makes the point that the impact of this stereotype can be seen in judicial perceptions about employment discrimination cases against women, in family law, and in the treatment of women lawyers by male judges, attorneys, and other court personnel. In contrast to this stereotype of woman as Mary is the stereotype of woman as Eve, the unchaste, eternal temptress. Schrafran maintains that this latter view of woman can seriously bias the outcome of certain cases in which "the lessening but continued adherence to the stereotype of the rape victim as temptress is still a serious problem."[6]

From *Sexism and the Legal Profession*, written by Albie Sachs and Joan Hoff Wilson, Schrafran offers a passage that she believes describes the parameters and contradiction of these stereotypes:

> The law in the United States represents the epitome of the stereo-
> typic masculine characteristics of rational thinking, competitive-
> ness, aggressiveness, strength, and seriousness. Conversely feminine
> or affiliative characteristics are routinely described as those of
> emotional responses, weakness, delicacy, gentleness, and frivol-
> ity. . . . This . . . male image of women as somehow morally superior
> yet . . . intellectually inferior, has forced women through the ages
> to live with contradiction, with an internal discord and confusion
> about their true nature.[7]

Therefore, for the man who called me the sexy broad, if I wasn't
Mary at home caring for my children and attending to domestic responsibility, then I had to be Eve, sent by someone behind the scenes to
seduce the male business owners out of their money. Whatever stories,
whatever narratives with their symbolic languages, whatever rituals
with their symbolic actions had formed this man's limited image of
women, these were in cataclysmic encounter with the symbolic language that had formed my images of myself as a woman.

What myths formed my inner images that gave me the vision and
impetus to walk that shaky and uncertain road of a woman living in
two worlds? When I was growing up, I certainly inherited, as I am sure
many people did, the countless images of the cowboy hero riding
around on his horse, wearing a ten-gallon hat and two six-shooters,
bringing justice to the world by killing bad men and rescuing fair ladies
in distress. In fact, I was determined to marry a cowboy when I grew
up.

In addition to the cowboy hero images, I also had two cherished
fairy tale books packed with images of brave knights and defenseless
princesses. I recognized at an early age that the only hope for Rapunzel
and Snow White and Cinderella lay in the courage and skill of their
rescuing knights.

Besides marrying a cowboy and being a rescued fairy-tale princess,
I also collected other stories of real people from the past and the present
who carried heroic images. As a young girl, I admired Florence Night-
ingale for her courageous life as a nurse, Saint Teresa of Avila for her
spirituality and aggressiveness, and Harriet Tubman for her efforts to
bring slaves to freedom in the North on the Underground Railway and
for serving as a spy behind Confederate lines during the Civil War.
While in high school, I admired Rosa Parks, the black woman who
refused to sit in the "Blacks Only" section of an Alabama bus, and
Eleanor Roosevelt, who labored for humanitarian causes. When I at-

tended college, Coretta Scott King and Sandra Day O'Connor inspired me. Most recently, I find myself admiring Mildred Maguire, the Catholic housewife from Northern Ireland who, together with Betty Williams, won the Nobel Peace Prize in 1977 after organizing the Peace People Movement to combat violence in their land.

I believe we need to recover a more accurate scriptural image of Eve and Mary. Is Eve, as presented in Genesis 3, really the seducer of all humankind, or is she, like Adam, simply one who made a choice and experienced the consequences? Rather than accept the image of Mary as Virgin Mother, an image created by generations of interpretation by a gender-biased culture, why not reflect on Mary as she is presented in the first chapter of Luke. There she is the first disciple—the one who was the first to say yes to the Word of God. We need to see the Mary who, as a young unmarried girl, said yes to pregnancy in defiance of social custom in a culture that was capable of stoning women to death for adultery. We need to hear the Mary who, in her hymn of praise, speaks against those in power and speaks up for the lowly and the oppressed. We need to encounter the *real* Mary, the one who pondered in her heart the events of her life, the woman who is Source of Wisdom.

We need to know the image of Mary given by Robert McAfee Brown in his book, *Unexpected News: Reading the Bible with Third World Eyes*. He tells us that the peasants of South America image Mary not as a queen in an embroidered gown sitting on a throne, but, rather, as a barefoot girl dressed in rags and living in the *barrios* with the poor, a girl who will lead the oppressed and the hungry to a better life.[8]

In a "Once upon a Future Time," what kind of rituals could replace the Homecoming pageant that I described? Here is what I would like to see: a ritual that celebrates that young women of today are more than just fairy-tale princesses waiting to be rescued by handsome princes, a ritual that symbolizes the deeply compassionate, caring, peace-loving side of our young men (a ritual, incidentally, that might even allow them to cry if they should receive a special honor). I believe that we need to celebrate the triumph of the spirit wherever and in whatever degree it occurs.

Thinking in terms of a possible high school scenario, I envision a ritual celebrated before the entire student body that gives recognition to a young woman who, because she made some unwise choices, becomes pregnant her sophomore year, gives birth before her junior year, struggles to keep her baby, works part-time, and studies when she can. She finally graduates at the end of her senior year with a low class rank, but for her, graduation is a personal triumph. She deserves recognition.

Or, we might have a ritual that celebrates the young man who, after five shaky years of drug use, finally goes straight and graduates in the lower third of his class. He misses achieving high academic and athletic honors, but his is a great personal success. He deserves celebration.

We need to celebrate people like the young friend of mine who has been confined to a wheelchair since he was hit by a school bus in fourth grade. He befriends everyone he meets, and as I hurry by on healthy legs, he never fails to ask me, "And how are you today, Mrs. B?" He will never be a heroic athlete or a romantic idol. He will, however, manage to graduate with the rest of his class.

This is where my encounter with myth in the fall of 1988 has led me. I envision the rituals of the future. We need rituals and myths that address themselves to the average person, to the lowly, to those who could never measure up to being number one. We need ritual and myth that establish a social norm other than the princess/macho hero syndrome. We need a symbolic language that proclaims the essential dignity and worth of all human beings, both male and female, and their struggle in life, regardless of their rating on the ladder of success.

1. Joseph Martos, *Doors to the Sacred* (New York: Doubleday and Company, 1982), 20.

2. Joseph Campell, *The Power of Myth* (New York: Doubleday, 1987).

3. Leonel Mitchell, *The Meaning of Ritual* (New York: Paulist Press, 1977).

4. Kevin Seasoltz, "Spirituality for Liturgical Ministers," Liturgical Workshop at St. John's University (Collegeville, MN: July 1987).

5. Lyn Hect Schrafran, "How Stereotypes about Women Influence Judges," *Outlook* (January/February 1989): 11.

6. As quoted in Schrafran, 14.

7. As quoted in Schrafran, 11.

8. Robert McAfee Brown, *Unexpected News: Reading the Bible with Third World Eyes* (Philadelphia: Westminster Press, 1984), 87.

3.

How Myths Define Women

Let us, as wise women, be a part of this re-mythologizing process, and let us be the teachers, trainers, educators.
THE REVEREND SUSAN MAETZOLD MOSS
Theological Insights, April 21, 1989

Growing Up with Fairy Tales

Gertrud Mueller Nelson

A long time ago, before TV, before the drip-dry shirt, perhaps even before the automatic washer and dryer, I was a little girl and I looked forward to Tuesdays. At that time Tuesday was also known as ironing day. And on Tuesdays my mother, one or another of my sisters or brothers, and I would go down to the basement with a great basket of fresh-smelling linens to iron. Did my mother like to iron? I don't know. I only know that I liked it when my mother ironed because if we quietly handed her the next item to be pressed and put what was freshly ironed into its appropriate pile, we might gently coax to life the mood she slipped into on an ironing day. It was a storytelling mood— one that we carefully prompted and encouraged with little suggestions, hoping that she'd soon begin. In due time, as the rhythm of ironing set in, she would indeed feel a story coming on.

My mother was—and still is—a very good storyteller and her repertoire never ceases to astonish. Most of her stories she knew by heart and, though Tuesdays were not the only occasions when we could coax a story from her, I rather suspect that telling stories while ironing was a way to transform a task and tap the dreamy, reflective place to where the mind retreats during routine tasks, looking for the gifts of another world.

It was also clear that, on some level, my mother believed deeply in the truth and power of myths and fairy tales, because they were a rich part of our heritage as we grew. From her we learned the Greek myths, a sizable collection of fairy tales from all the world, the legends of the saints, stories from Hebrew Scripture, Gospel stories as they occurred in their seasons, and a bonus smattering of holy legends that never quite made it as far as the Gospels. And as well as this oral tradition, from her, and from my father with his nose for good books, I received, at a young age, my very own volume of the complete Grimms and a fat, handsome volume of Greek myths.

I never outgrew these stories or these two books but rather steadily grew into them. They were nourishing fare in my childhood and adolescence, the pure, unobstructed view into mystery. I drew from these books as a primary source in my teaching and used my students as an excuse to reenter that world with them. They were exactly the stories I told and the books that I read to my own children and which they read and continue to read in their young adulthood.

But there comes a time when we are no longer simple enough to see our visions with a clear eye. Then I found Carl Gustav Jung's psychology a useful lens through which to peer into the visions once more.

After some work at the Jung Institute in Zurich, I was asked by our local Jung Society to talk on myths and fairy tales. What began rather formally as a four-part presentation grew into more than a decade of women's gatherings in my living room. I drew a great deal of help from Jung's insight and most especially from his student, a seminal analyst of myths and fairy tales, Marie-Louise von Franz.

We began, on those Wednesday mornings, with tea and talk during which time we became acquainted and warmed as a group. Then we gathered in the living room in a circle. We listened to a story. I followed with an "oral essay" on what I had learned from the story from my readings and especially from my personal experience. The presentation was followed by discussion—and sometimes simply by long periods of silence. How surprised we often were, deeply touched, amazed—but mostly greatly comforted—that the heroic lives described in these stories grappled with the issues we faced in our own lives. So none of us, living lives of unspoken questions in our kitchens and work cubicles, were really so alone. Our struggles were uniquely ours, but they were also the struggles that belonged to the development of the feminine. Women everywhere shared our wounds, failed their trials, but behold, they also were given the means to heal and transform.

The fairy tales carried us through our relationships, lent meaning to our loves and our losses, shed light on our sexual confusion, helped us to mother and raise our daughters and sons. We grew clearer about the nature and meaning of the feminine and about our own natures as women. And we discovered that conflicting styles of living out our femininity and the wounds of fate have always been part of the human condition. We felt curiously joined to those who peopled our stories, to each other, to all women, and to the feminine wherever we found it.

Speaking for myself, I came to realize that the variations and details of my personal life formed a journey no less heroic than those described in our stories—inimitable, unique, astonishing.

Though our search began with a woman's focus, we soon learned that the development of the feminine was also part of a man's unfolding of his inner feminine side. And there were stories to help us understand the heroic journeys of the men in our lives.

From Wednesday to Wednesday at ten in the morning and year after year, these men saw us grow braver and more understanding of them. Certainly some of them, hearing the stories that especially moved us, also found them useful in understanding us better. What's more, we all learned that it was not just women who were wounded and in need of healing; the feminine values in men and in our masculine society were also in danger and in need of healing. And so it was that many men were also introduced to the neglected feminine side of their own selves.

For just as yin and yang spin and tumble into one another and are never static, and just as each is inoculated with a spot of its opposite, so men and women are inoculated with a bit of their opposite side. Men, though they may be assertive, active and dynamic, are also touched with a "feminine" element inside them, where they find their qualities of feeling and relatedness, their imagination or their gifts of empathy. And women, though they may be more comfortable with an interiority, with their intuitive knowledge, with receptivity and interpersonal relationships, are touched with the "masculine" energies that allow them to create order, make decisions, take the initiative or function practically in the outside world. In a right relationship between men and women each of them has a right relationship to his or her inner soul—he to his inner feminine side and she to her inner masculine side. These qualities will be their guides in the creation of whole and healthy personalities. The words "masculine" and "feminine," then, are to be understood as qualities found within women and men in turn, but are not to be mistaken as descriptive of "males" or "females."

The wisdom we gleaned from these tales, like a pebble dropped
n a pond, sent waves out in circles and touched people far beyond the
Vednesday experience. We had scratched something powerful, useful
nd attractive to people of both sexes and all ages. I suspected as much
vhen our group—now jamming the living room, filling the dining room
nd spilling over into the kitchen—included my daughter with some
f her friends crouched on the floor between feet and folding chairs,
quiet as mice. They claimed a bad case of "senioritis" as their excuse
or needing to play hooky from school and sneak back to the house to
e with us. Their senioritis recurred magically on a number of those
Vednesday mornings, though now with the blessing of their curious
English teacher, who only asked for their oral reports on what they
earned there. The Wednesday group finally outgrew its space and the
uxury of free weekdays was curtailed by economic realities. My own
vork continued with fairy tales and grew into workshops and seminars.

I found, in the sharing of fairy tales with people around the coun-
ry, a great interest in an extended unfolding of the truth these stories
old. They found that the issues of our feminine revolution needed
edefinition as a feminine *evolution* with the promise of healing. Line
y line, the thought we broke open taught us about ourselves, the
truggle for feminine value, the human condition.

Once upon a time there was a certain miller . . . Once upon a time,
n a far-off castle, there lived a King and a Queen . . . Once upon a time
airy tales were told not just to children but were shared among people
f all ages, because the wisdom in fairy tales is ageless and their age is
imeless. That is why they so often begin with those words "Once upon
time"—which is to say in a time-out-of-time, or in timeless eternity,
n *illo tempore*, in a time beyond history. "Once upon a time" heads us
ff to a realm of archetypal truth and mythic reality.

In our rationality and logic we often find it difficult to enter into
nythic reality. As adults, we have cultivated our intellects to deal mainly
vith the rational world. We rather like to think that mystery or magic
s so much childish nonsense. But leave it to a child to come up with a
vay to understand the validity of mythic reality. This is a definition
or myth that I learned from my youngest daughter when she was
bout five. She was being tested by a school psychologist to see if she
vas ready to attend kindergarten. He asked her some questions to
etermine something about her verbal skills and that evening he phoned
s to tell us of their conversation. He had asked her:

"Annika, do your parents read you stories?"

"Stories? Oh yes. My papa tells us Piggle-Wiggle stories and my mama reads us Greek myths."

"Greek myths! Really? What are myths?"

"Oh, you know. Mythology? Those are stories"—and she paused—
"stories that aren't true on the outside. But they *are* true on the inside!

This definition seems a useful tool. It indicates that there is an inner
truth just as much as there is an outer truth. It indicates that inner truth
and outer truth are probably equal in value though one lives in the dark
and the other in the light. Each truth speaks its own language and must
be understood in its own realm.

But isn't it the fate of the human condition that the very process
of becoming adult is to work so long at making sense of outer truth and
its reality that we often give it a greater value? We certainly give it more
time. This is the realm where we take things literally. We place these
realities into historical context. We hand them over to science to meas
ure and test. Preoccupied with outer realities, we may forget the inner
world altogether—forget its mythic language and how to understand
it. Out of sight, out of mind. But, for all that, still alive and well.

For our mythic, inner reality never gives up pursuing us. Now it
just has to try harder. Aiming to get our attention, it pops out in "slip.
of the tongue." It dresses up in the clothes of the people we passionately
admire and wears the disguise of those we fear, mistrust or reject. It
enriches our creativity or petrifies our growth. It rides heavily on our
shoulders and whispers in our ear, begging to be made conscious and
to be taken seriously by influencing our habits or burdening us with
symptoms, fears and gnawing guilts. It fills us with longing and haunt
us with the desire to search for "something more." All night it spins our
wonderful and horrible tales fashioned only for us, producing fantastic
images, offering useful insight, never giving up.

But since dream language—or mythic language—tells us a truth
which is not literal but inner and since we have lost touch with our inner
world, we cannot receive our messages. We fail to take its wisdom to
heart until we can hear that symbolic language, know the level on which
it speaks and can translate its meaning.

Mythic language, then, for complicated adults (*never for chil
dren*), may need translation and pondering if its wisdom is to soar
through our guarded hearts and hand up nourishment to our outer lives
If we ignore our inside truth, we will keep on honoring and blaming
our inner heroes and our inner enemies by projecting them onto per
sons or countries or races of the outside world. We will be riddled with
neurotic symptoms and plagued with anxieties. We will wrongly inter
pret what is inner and personal to be true as outer and literal and will

consume compulsively, only to wonder why our hunger is never stilled. Finally we will have rejected the gift whose purpose is to lead us to healing and wholeness. Mythic language is a thread we can follow to our very transformation and redemption.

In the old days, the spinning of stories—by open fires, while husking the corn, while knitting socks—was a kind of spiritual occupation or a form of religious search. Just as we might follow a thread through our dreams and learn to unravel meaning there and gain enlightenment, we can also follow the threads that are spun out in the great collective dreams of myth and fairy tale. For a fairy tale is the dream language of a whole culture. Fairy tales are our own big dreams. The heroes and villains, who have paraded across pillows everywhere and who have taken up residence in the secret corners of our waking dreams to live out untold dramas, rise to the surface in the fairy tale. There these dream folk, now distilled of personal distortions, become the truths and symbols which belong to us all. In fairy tales they speak the colorful language of the soul of a people. They teach us about our culture and they return to us essential psychic facts about ourselves.

Unlike allegories, fables or cautionary tales, which may have been created to form a culture, fairy tales are more like rumblings from a deep, unconscious source within the culture. They often show the culture for what it is or forewarn and predict. They also contain a wisdom about the human condition. Devoid of self-consciousness, fairy tales focus on the realm in which we live but give us a perspective from the bottom up.

Fairy tales often begin on the surface; they make some ordinary comment on what is going on in the ordinary, surface world. Then, suddenly, the surface gives way and we are plunged down the well into the inner world. With the abandon of a child, we tumble, unable to brace ourselves, and find ourselves in a mysterious place. Now we are in an enchanted forest, or we walk on the bottom of the sea, or animals speak to us, and we can understand. In this place are revealed to us our heroic duties and the dreadful trials we must endure so that change can be effected and a deliverance set in motion. From the bottom up or from the inside out, we have a new view of our conscious world by encountering the grand projected images of the unconscious.

Just as in the interpretation of our dreams, we take to heart all the characters who people the drama. We carry traits of both the hero *and* the villain, the kind mother *and* the witch, the princess *and* the prince, the fool *and* the wise one, the frog *and* the king. We become more human and more whole as we meet ourselves in every character portrayed and own them as aspects of ourselves—crowns, warts and all.

Because fairy tales contain powerful truths about the human condition, many of them, with tenacity and uncanny persistence, turn up, theme and variation, in vastly different cultures. The stories seem to say that certain truths are everyone's reality, no matter where we live. We are all sisters and brothers in our journey toward wholeness, and the stories breathe new life into the mysteries of our shared condition to make it comprehensible and to lend us the courage to lift up our eyes and see one another as fellow pilgrims on a holy road.

So we crack open our stories and enter "a fairy tale world" but quickly discover that this world offers no "retreat from reality," nor does it invite us to a world of shining bliss. Rather, anguish and darkness are the fairy tale's prevailing tone—the anguish of a lost paradisiacal happiness and the inevitable darkness that enters every life. In darkness and anguish, we stumble upon the fevers of the soul or the fevers of the culture. More often than not, there is an enchantment which is not a positive transformation—not enchanting at all, as we like to use that word—but a stunting or maiming of the hero or the culture.

In the darkness and pain of the story we engage our own "stuck" places, the blocks, the wounds, the fears, the passions, the possibilities. We learn that only anguish and a *dis*enchantment can transform us. Disguises are pulled away: the kind mother is also a witch, the generous man is a devil, the frog is a prince, the scullery maid a princess. Only in disenchantment and in lowliness will the hero become real. In engaging the frogginess of ourselves, transformation is made possible. Dressed in our scullery rags and not in our ball gowns, we will come to recognize who we are. Seated in ashes, we can be connected to our noble nature. In fairy tales the hero is transformed to what he or she was always meant to be—but was unable to become until hard work and heroic deeds had been accomplished.

After sorrow and heroic deeds we arrive in that paradoxical place that lies between illusion and disillusionment, between enchantment and disenchantment, a place of tension that points toward wholeness—which also means health, holiness—and the promise of redemption.

Fairy tales, for all their economy of language and symbolic form, often reveal a kind of symmetry. They diagnose the problem for us. They plunge us into the crisis, often filled with chaos and darkness, and the mandate to perform daring tasks or suffer a deep wound. But in the midst of the dark predicament is revealed a prescription for healing. In suffering, the hero works toward this healing. And when the story ends with the symbolism of a marriage and of perfect love, this can be understood as something profound: the dualism of masculine and feminine have transcended polarization and have come to a place where opposites no longer elude each other or work against each other or misunderstand each other. Rather the crisis of opposites is resolved and the conflict is healed. What has been incompatible now merges in loving empathy. Such a marriage is the ultimate place of wholeness and the story uses the biological differences between male and female to speak symbolically about psychic and spiritual opposites or polarities. This is a mythic marriage, not necessarily literal—a union beyond gender. This is the overlapping of any and all opposites to create a single, new reality—the hope of every human soul—where opposites, though separate, become equal, balanced, shared and fruitful.

It seems a mighty final chord—a neat wrap-up, a comforting resolution. And a story in symbols can do that, only to return us to the fray of our own lives and to that disordered chorus of those who have lost their gods and think they can invent themselves. We go back to the struggle between parents and children, between old values and new, between village and city, inside and outside, masculine and feminine— to learn again and again that neither is valid if it excludes the other. Both realities are at once a constriction and a ticket to freedom. Only in their marriage, in perfect love and community, with massive infusions of grace, can we work for the true Kingdom: that third way, the unitive vision that accepts all contradictions, aware of everything, judgmental of no one.

Through the Looking Glass

Geri Giebel Chavis

The relationship between myths and women's roles through the ages is far from simple. Myths certainly have had a profound effect on women's roles, their behavior in these roles, and the self-image accompanying these roles. Through generating memorable impressions and stereotypes, myths remain with us long after we cease to believe in the gods or heroes these myths describe. Moreover, folklore, religious texts, fairy tales, literary works, and, in our own time, mass media act as powerful vehicles that perpetuate myths across the generations. Yet, these cultural conveyors modify myths as well, and myths themselves have even been defined as "approximation(s) to Truth" or "working hypotheses destined one day to be abandoned."[1] It also seems likely that women's changing experiences in conjunction with changing role expectations gradually forge new myths.

Created in patriarchal societies, ancient myths focusing on women's experience are stories primarily told by men defining acceptable and punishable behaviors for the female community. The roles emerging from these myths tend to be strongly colored by male bias, ambivalence, need, and fear. Thus, our time-honored myths delineating and affecting women's lives tend to be characterized by ambivalence. Most of the popular myths saturating Western culture have focused on women's experience in relation to males or family: mother, wife, lover, daughter and sister. In our own time, as more and more women writers are taking control of the myth-making process and envisioning ancient female heroic figures, the roles of friend, artist, quester, and woman alone are gaining prominence, and the past images affecting role expectations are being challenged.

The ambivalence characterizing myths emerging from patriarchal culture is particularly striking in the mother figure. On the most profound level, the duality of woman's nature found in these myths reflects primordial reactions to the Earth Mother. The Great Mother embodies images of good and evil, pleasure and pain, for she reflects both the love felt for the creator of life and the deep fear inspired by death, which inevitably follows the gift of life. The great ancient goddesses—Gaia, Isis, and Demeter—capture in their essence the birth-death-rebirth cycle: the promise, fertility, and sustenance of spring and summer along with the desolation and betrayal of winter. In fairy tales, the same duality is represented by the fairy godmother and the evil stepmother. As the basic provider of food and security, mother also has the power to withhold these necessities or poison those in her care.

In relation to sons, the mythic mother can be a self-sacrificer or a castrater threatening her child's manhood. She is the docile, loving mother whose child is her destiny, the "Mater Dolorosa" of the Bible—Mary, mother of Jesus, Rachel, mother of Benjamin, and Anna, mother of the Nazarite, Samuel. Yet, she is also the possessive mother who cannot let go of her children: Aphrodite with her adored son, Cupid, or the modern mythic figure, Sophie Portnoy, who distorts her son's sexual development. In her most evil incarnation, mother is the raging, terrible Earth deity, the desperate Medea annihilating her own children, the jealous Hera murdering the illegitimate progeny of Zeus, or the legendary Lamia, the snake-vampire-lady who sucks the life-blood of children.

As the parent of daughters, mother also reveals her mixed nature. Standing alone in ancient times in its emphasis on the mother-daughter bond and the power of this alliance in the universe is the Demeter-Persephone myth, one associated with the most holy rite of worship for both men and women in Pre-Hellenic Greece. Carl Jung and his followers have helped to transmit this myth into the modern imagination and to incorporate it into the practice of psychology. And today, many women exploring their role as mothers of daughters, are reworking this myth, weaving it into their poems, fiction, and memoirs. Demeter is the adoring mother of Persephone who reluctantly becomes queen of the underworld after being abducted by Hades. The lasting love between mother and daughter is powerfully conveyed in the seasonal metaphors of the story. When Demeter loses her daughter, her grief becomes the frost of winter, but when mother and daughter reunite, spring and summer bring joy and renewed life to all humankind. Like other mother figures, Demeter too has a dual nature—gentle, beautiful and blossoming when her daughter is with her, but hag-like, rageful and destructive when her daughter resides in Hades.

In the middle of our own century, the ancient dichotomy within the mother image once again became evident, as the "Myth of Total Mothering" takes hold. During this era, ironically, writers and orators sanctify motherhood, while mental health experts repeatedly identify the over-involved, dominant mother as the primary source of her children's psychological problems. While women are being convinced to take on the mother-housewife role in earnest, they are also blamed for doing their jobs too thoroughly. The bi-fold nature of Mother at this time is vividly illustrated by the co-existence of highly sentimentalized Mother's Day cards and a widely read book by Philip Wylie called *Generation of Vipers* with its description of a disease called "Momism" and its scathing portraits of domineering mothers who blight their children's lives.[4]

The ambivalence inherent in the mother role is also evident in the wife image as it has been transmitted through myth. The mythic portraits of Wife that still retain power for us today reflect a split between idealizations and the disillusionment that follows an unattainable dream. Like the ideal mother, the ideal wife is submissive, loving and faithful. Like the terrible mother, the domineering, shrewish wife is feared, ridiculed and abhorred.

We see clear examples of the idealized wife role in the biblical portrait of a "woman of valor" from Proverbs and in Homer's famous portrait of Penelope in *The Odyssey*. Beautiful Penelope is the ever-faithful, long-waiting, and virtuous wife who earns the praise and deserves the faithfulness of her heroic mate. The wife described in Proverbs 31 is this and more. Her principal feature is the good she brings her husband, for she is not only pure, wise, compassionate, and charitable, but also so hardworking and clever that she brings amazing prosperity to her household.

The ideal wife in the nineteenth century becomes not so much a woman of valor as "the angel in the house," who provides her husband with a moral example. She rescues her husband from his lustful nature creating a spiritual haven from the gritty, materialistic work world the man encounters on the outside. In order to sustain this domestic paradise, the wife is expected to live up to a set of behaviors defined in a powerful myth called the "Cult of True Womanhood." She "must provide in the home a climate of peace and happiness, of self-sacrificing love and self-effacing gentility in order to 'save the family.'"[2]

In contrast to the ideal wife, a well-known negative embodiment of the wife figure is Hera, spouse of the philandering Zeus. While in ancient, pre-Hellenic Greece she is viewed as the glorious protector of marriage, symbol of fertility, and guardian of childbirth, in her later, more well-known manifestations in patriarchal Hellenic Greece, she is seen primarily as the jealous, troublesome wife. To survive, this later version of Hera pretends submission to Zeus, while retaining her pride and ability to act—through deceptive, subversive behaviors that temporarily undermine her husband's power. Hera's double-faced quality and her power in pretended weakness find counterparts throughout literature and popular culture, from Nora in Ibsen's *A Doll's House* to the wacky wife in the enormously popular "I Love Lucy" television series.

Like the wife, the love-goddess combines positive and negative qualities. She is, first and foremost, the ultimate male fantasy, golden-haired or with exotic raven tresses, light of foot and ready to prepare a feast of pleasure when her loved one beckons. In her innocent form, she is a maiden awaiting her prince, rewarded finally with marriage at the end of the tale. She is Rapunzel, Sleeping Beauty, Cinderella, and Snow White. But she is also Queen Esther of the Old Testament, whose beauty and grace dazzle the monarch of a powerful nation and enable her to become the savior of her people. The virgin love-goddess is woman on a pedestal, Pygmalion's Galatia, but she is also, in her most supremely spiritual form, Mary, the second or redeemed Eve, Virgin Bride of God and Mother of Jesus. From the pen of Lord Byron, she is the woman who "walks in beauty like the night, of cloudless climes and starry skies," with a heart "whose love is innocent!"[3]

An equally pervasive manifestation of the love-goddess is the not-so-innocent but powerfully alluring mistress. She is Aphrodite, goddess of beauty and love; Helen of Troy, whose face "launched a thousand ships"; the enchanting Moon Goddess Cynthia who captivates the mortal Endymion; and "La Belle Dame Sans Merci" present in medieval ballad and later popularized by Romantic poet, John Keats. She is also Pandora and her biblical counterpart, Eve, irresistible females whose actions bring sin and death into the world. The beautiful woman without mercy is a contradictory blend of loving submissiveness and dangerous power. The duality of her nature is perhaps explained by the fact that beauty of immortal proportions is tremendously attractive, providing men with power and pleasure, yet also mysterious and something to be feared. The evil that the love-goddess brings seems to reflect her male admirers' fears of their own uncontrollable desires or enthrallment.

In her most evil form, the love-goddess is temptress and betrayer. She is Circe or Siren in the world of Homer or the Philistine Delilah, betrayer of Samson and his people. She is the serpent lady, concealing her true identity under a beautiful, superficial exterior. In her more luckless manifestations, she is the violated maiden, woman set apart from her pure sisters, the scarlet whore living on the fringes of society.

Like other female roles, the daughter role, with its stereotypic features, evolved from divergent myths. The stories of Ruth, Persephone, and Athena provide archetypal patterns that have helped shape this role. Like the biblical heroine Ruth, an image of daughter that still has a strong hold on the popular imagination embodies traits of patience, self-sacrifice, dependability, and compassion. It is, for example, daughters, rather than sons, who are normally expected to care for younger or disabled siblings and aged parents.

Like Ruth who leaves her own parents to "cleave" to her mother-in-law in a land of her spouse's people, Persephone, too, experiences the age-old rhythm of attachment and separation that have long characterized the daughter's role. Persephone is obedient, loving, and very attached to her adoring mother, yet she undergoes the inevitable process that moves her from innocence to experience. When she wanders in the meadow away from mother, is abducted by Hades, and ultimately eats the pomegranate seeds in underworld regions, she relinquishes forever the exclusive tie to mother. Even after she is joyously reunited with her sorrowing mother, for three months of every year she must return to her wifely throne in Hades' kingdom. As reflected in Persephone's story, the typical daughter's role is to juggle the staying and the leaving, to maintain loving connection with the maternal hearth, while forging new relationships in her adult world.

In contrast to Persephone, Athena is the prototype of a daughter image that has not been prevalent until contemporary times. Athena is the tough-minded, active daughter who emerges full-armored from the head of Zeus after he has swallowed her natural mother. She is goddess of wisdom, arts, and sciences, a divinity of defensive war but not a lover of violence, and presider over both typically "masculine" and "feminine" occupations. In her diversity of roles and uniquely motherless origin, she is the androgynous, autonomous daughter, a product of paternal imagination or intellect. She is perhaps the prototype for the tomboy stereotype or the high-achieving female offspring who functions as her father's surrogate son.

The sister role, less prevalent in mythology than the above roles, has been tainted with myths that emphasize rivalry for male favor and attention. Three classic examples come to mind: Psyche and the jealous sisters who complicate her life with Eros, Rachel and Leah competing for Jacob's favor and engaging in a childbearing contest with high stakes, and Cinderella, victimized by her stepsisters yet ultimately triumphant because of her superior feminine charms. Myths like these have saturated the popular imagination to this day with stories of strife, not loving kinship, between sisters. However, in nineteenth-century works of fiction by such women writers as Jane Austen and Louisa May Alcott, we begin to get a more balanced and positive picture of the sisterly bond. And today, women writers like Alice Walker in *The Color Purple*[5] and Nancy Thayer in *Three Women at the Waters' Edge* are telling fuller, more complex stories about sisters.[6]

Like models of sisterly affection, models of female friendship are virtually nonexistent in Greco-Roman myth and biblical texts. From ancient times, friendship was seen as being for men only. Freud, along with numerous other intellectual leaders before him, perpetuated this myth by suggesting that women were too child-like, unstable, and prone to petty jealousies to maintain true friendships. Today, however, we know from historical and biographical documents of the eighteenth and nineteenth centuries that enduring and loving relationships between women were indeed quite common. Today's myth about friendship actually constitutes a reversal of the ancient notions. While impassioned descriptions of male friendship among heterosexual men have almost disappeared from view in literature and popular culture, researchers like Lillian Rubin are revealing that women form and maintain deeper, more intimate friendships than men.[7] According to Louise Bernikow in her book, *Among Women*, women's conversations among themselves contain emotional content foreign to most males, who are never privy to these heartfelt talks, a fact that helps explain why male myth-makers have not concerned themselves with the substance of women's friendships.[8]

Like the female friends in a room alone, Woman-Alone or Artist-Scholar-Quester is a role that has been defined *not* in relation to men or family life. In this category, women are defined in much the same way men have been defined, that is, in relation to God, the universe, the society at large, or themselves. We may also name this role Woman-Intact or Spiritual Virgin, the word virgin being used in its original etymological sense as having integrity or belonging to oneself. A primary ancient prototype of this role is Artemis, the virgin huntress, cunning protector of her own integrity, and chief goddess worshipped by the Amazons. Other mythic figures helping to define this role are Athena; the questing, resourceful Psyche who goes through rites of passage to become a Soul; the Vestal Virgins; the biblical heroines, Judith and Deborah, who were sages and deliverers of their people; and saints like Catherine of Alexandria and Joan of Arc.

This strong woman-alone figure has posed a threat that is evident in myths and stereotypes that degrade her. In her negative manifestations, she is the pathetic spinster, the dreaded old maid of the popular card game; the bluestocking or "scribbler" vilified for her high-flown literary aspirations; the man-hating, counter-cultural lesbian; or the witch burned at the stake.

While these unflattering stereotypes represent attempts to curb her power, the woman-alone, as artist or scholar, has a voice and presence that grows stronger every day. Through her books, poems, memoirs, and fiction, she is re-visioning old myths or fashioning new ones. She is analyzing old roles and the reasons for their survival, defining new roles and attempting to integrate a variety of roles. In reflecting upon what it means to be a woman today, she is addressing the phenomenon of the Superwoman myth that evolved in the 1970s and 1980s. The Superwoman reflects a merging of several roles described in ancient and modern myth and seems to originate from a desire to have it all—beauty, brains, a successful career, leadership qualities, a fulfilling marriage, and healthy, well-adjusted children.

In her exploration of choices, Woman-Alone is the Existential Quester, a role formerly reserved primarily for the male hero. As quester, she is claiming the powerful ancient goddesses as muses or her literary foremothers as mentors.

Two nineteenth-century mentors who planted the seeds for today's creative blossoming are Emily Bronte and Emily Dickinson, both of whom protected their inner life while finding their voice in poetry. In a poem called "Often Rebuked," Bronte writes, "I'll walk where my own nature would be leading. It vexes me to choose another guide." Emily Dickinson tells us in her poetry that "The Soul selects her own Society—Then shuts the Door—To her divine majority—Present no more—."[10]

A twentieth-century voice that dares to defy can be heard in Gaë De La Rozière's poem, "La Poeta—Dream." Here we find a poet so sure of her own creative powers that she can walk naked in sandals and red socks amidst shocked crowds at an airport, "Firm in her/Flesh/Woman."[1]

Another contemporary poet, Linda Pastan, also suggests defiance as she explores old roles in a poem called "Marks." Aware of all the "grades" she receives from husband and children on a daily basis, the female persona concludes with the message: "Wait 'til they learn, I'm dropping out."[12]

Like Pastan, Erica Jong in "Woman Enough" depicts a struggle with old roles, when she bluntly states her dilemma between home-making and creating art:

> I wish there were not a choice;
> I wish I could be two women.
> I wish the days could be longer.
> But they are short.
> So I write while
> the dust piles up.[13]

Moving even further beyond the traditional, Nikki Giovanni, in her poem "Woman," creates fresh metaphors as she describes a woman trying on new roles. The woman likens herself to a blade of grass, a robin singing, a spider spinning a web, a book, and a bulb. For each new self-image she chooses, she recognizes that the man in her life is refusing to play a complementary role, yet rather than despair, she concludes her quest on a positive note:

> she decided to become
> a woman
> and though he still refused
> to be a man
> she decided it was all
> right.[14]

Alice Koller's autobiographical book, *An Unknown Woman*, provides us with one final striking example of a woman trying to shed the old roles and figure out what kind of woman she is, without the myths, stereotypes and all that their influence entails. Living in an isolated area after leaving all her old occupations and acquaintances behind, the writer recounts a struggle whose essence is suggested in the following excerpt:

> Each thing I do during the course of a day is something I've been told to do, or taught to do. I have to replace all of it with what I choose to do. . . .
>
> So I'll wear something if it's clean and will keep me warm. I'll try not to think whether it fits or is without patches or holes or is too long or too short. Except, the color will matter. I'll play with colors in all sorts of ways, but some I will not have together. I'm sure of my sense of color.

So soon. It's my first clear judgment, *my* judgment. A very tiny step I take. How will knowing that I trust my eye for color take me to knowing how I want to live my life? The chasm stretches beneath me.[15]

While Koller's chasm image suggests an empty abyss and expanses of unknown territory, today's women writers are populating this territory with new self-definitions and new myths by which to live. Certainly, the definition of myth as "approximation to Truth," a working hypothesis destined to be modified or surpassed in a new cultural context, is congruent with the activity of the artist-quester figure in our time. Alicia Ostriker, a contemporary poet/scholar who deliberately transforms ancient myths from a feminine viewpoint, describes the exciting enterprise of today's women myth-makers in this way:

> When she sings, when she dances, it is asking
> How to capture, how to keep, how to give back, unmasking
> Beauty, the seed to the sower, the gift to the giver—."[16]

1. Pierre L. Grimal, ed., *Larousse World Mythology* (New York: G. P. Putnam, 1965), 9.

2. Elizabeth Schussler Fiorenza, *In Memory of Her: A Feminist Theological Reconstruction of Christian Origins* (New York: Crossroad, 1984), 348.

3. Lord George Gordon Byron, "She Walks in Beauty," in *The Norton Anthology of English Literature, Vol. 2*, eds. M. H. Abrams, et al. (New York: Norton, 1986), 508-9.

4. Philip Wylie, *Generation of Vipers* (New York: Farrar and Rinehart, 1942).

5. Alice Walker, *The Color Purple* (New York: Harcourt Brace Jovanovich, 1982).

6. Nancy Thayer, *Three Women at the Water's Edge* (New York: Bantam, 1981).

7. Lillian Rubin, *Just Friends: The Role of Friendship in Our Lives* (New York: Harper and Row, 1985).

8. Louise Berkinov, *Among Women* (New York: Harper and Row, Colophon Books, 1980).

9. Emily Bronte, "Stanzas: Often Rebuked," in *The Norton Anthology of Literature by Women*, eds. Sandra M. Gilbert and Susan Gibar (New York: Norton and Co., 1985), 751-52.

10. Emily Dickinson, "The Soul Selects Her Own Society," in *Final Harvest*, selected by Thomas H. Johnson (Boston: Little, Brown & Co., 1890, 1961), 55.

11. Gaël De La Rozière, "La Poeta—Dream," in *Contemporary Women Poets: An Anthology of California Poets*, eds. Jennifer McDowell and M. Loventhal (San Jose, California: Merlin Press, 1977), 51.

12. Linda Pastan, "Marks," in *PM/AM: New and Selected Poems* (New York: Norton, 1982), 69.

13. Erica Jong, "Woman Enough," in *At the Edge of the Body* (New York: Holt, Rinehart & Winston, 1979), 71.

14. Nikki Giovanni, "Woman," in *Cotton Candy on a Rainy Day* (New York: William Morrow & Co., Inc., 1978), 71.

15. Alice Koller, *An Unknown Woman: A Journey to Self-Discovery* (New York: Bantam Books, 1981), 17-18.

16. Alicia Ostriker, "The Poet to Her Book," from "Message from the Sleeper at Hell's Mouth," in *A Woman under the Surface* (Princeton, NJ: Princeton University Press, 1982), 41.

4.

How Culture Forms Us

*Can we yet accept being a nation among nations,
not number one? Can we yet allow other nations
formerly seen as within our sphere of influence to
choose their own leaders, struggle through their
revolutions and wars of liberation . . . ?*

KAREN FITZPATRICK
Theological Insights, September 29, 1989

From Father's Daughter
to Babushka Lady

Louise O. Hiniker

The stories we tell each other about our lives are indeed holy. When we reflect on life events, recall significant relationships, and name critical turning points which shape our beliefs about who we are and who the Holy One is, we are engaged in experiential theology.

Forty-eight years ago, my mother named me Albina Louise. I carried the surname Osojnicki. My ancestors are Croatian and Slovenian Roman Catholics. My story describes how I moved from being a "Father's Daughter" to becoming a "Babushka Lady." The story has three parts: the description of some of my earliest memories and experiences of being female in a Slavic family, the recounting of important leave-takings from my family of origin and from communities in which I excelled as a father's daughter, and the description of my reconnecting with an alienated and buried feminine part of myself.

Some of my earliest childhood memories are of men in my family. My paternal grandfather, Mata, was a very gentle man. He used to make us laugh when we gathered on the back porch after dinner. I remember Grandpa as patriarch when each Christmas he slaughtered a suckling pig and each Easter a lamb. He took the life of these animals with great respect. He roasted them in the old-country style in his backyard in East Chicago, Indiana. This preparation took several days, and everyone helped. Our family feasts were tradition-filled celebrations.

My father is also named Mata, or Matt. I remember listening to

Dad imitate the calls of the bobwhite and thrush. He would whistle, and I would giggle and then name the bird he imitated. I always got them right. I also remember Dad's powerful hands. They were very hairy, and they always smelled of Lifebuoy soap. I felt safe when I was with him.

My Uncle Johnnie faithfully took me to Calpino Accordion School every Wednesday night for years. Afterwards, he would sing with me, like a Mario Lanza. When I was a toddler, I am told, Uncle Johnnie used to take me for walks and show me off to his friends. I believe I still have some body memory of his pride in me. He taught me that I contained something very special, the image of the Holy One that deserves to be reverenced and celebrated.

I was taught that God's name was "Boga." Boga was holy, and he looked something like Grandpa. We remembered Boga before we ate and before we went to sleep. I knew that Boga somehow was present in the tabernacle at Holy Trinity Croatian Church.

I remembered all this last summer when I spent a week at the Split Rock Arts Festival in Duluth, participating in a music seminar in which we improvised with our voices and with musical instruments. I improvised a song in Serbo-Croatian:

> Boga ide sada.
> Dice, dodgi.
> Slusaj, slusaj mali, slusaj cas.
> Boga ide me.

> The Holy One is coming now.
> Created ones, Come.
> Listen, listen, for in this moment.
> The Holy One comes.

I am grateful for the Boga I met through Grandpa Osojnicki, my father, and my Uncle Johnnie.

I also recall memories from the darker side of my childhood. These include, for example, the kind of attention my brother received from the paternal side of the family whom we visited on Sunday mornings after Mass. What a fuss when my brother showed up. Everyone and everything stopped to welcome him. He was treated like a prince, and I felt invisible.

Another memory from the dark side. Dad's five sisters were first-generation immigrants and still very nationalistic. Two of them resented that my father had married a "Krinica," a Slovenian woman. I watched my mother do whatever she could to placate her sisters-in-law. But in the end, Mom was never treated respectfully or affectionately by them. And as for me, I was my mother's daughter, another "Krinica." There was nothing I could do to change their attitude toward my mother or me.

So early in my life, I met the Good Father through three men but learned to feel inferior, to accept invisibility and rejection from the women in my family. Only later did I begin to understand the whole phenomenon of how my aunts had internalized their own sense of inferiority, of hurt and rage, and how they were projecting these onto my mother and me. They were sad victims themselves. In effect, they were teaching me what they had learned: to worship the male and the masculine, to hold contempt for the female and the feminine, (perhaps, the passive? weak? dependent?). To survive, I believe that I separated from that part of myself and learned to deny it. I made every effort to identify with what the culture saw as superior, becoming independent, developing purpose and direction, and achieving academic success.

And so I began a series of important leave-takings. I convinced my parents to enroll me at St. Joseph Academy in Lancaster, Pennsylvania, 750 miles from home. From age thirteen to seventeen, I studied, worked, and prayed. Life was ordered, almost monastic. I believed that Truth was known and Perfection was almost attainable.

Another dramatic leavetaking occurred in 1970 when I left East Chicago to come to Minnesota to attend graduate school. I actually left three communities at once. I left my extended family, Bishop Noll High School and my fellow teachers who were as idealistic as I was, and Sacred Heart parish where I was choir director and a CCD teacher and where we talked about Vatican II still with a great deal of hope. My identity was grounded in my family, my teaching, and my perception of myself as a woman of the church.

Graduate school at the University of Minnesota was a hard and dark experience. I was long overdue for an identity crisis and a faith crisis as well. I became aware of how much my self-definition had depended on the three communities I had left. I spent much of those two years depressed and spiritually confused. My world of meaning and religious symbols broke down. The Divinity of Christ, the Trinity, and the infallibility of the church had become irrelevant. I could no longer defend with any intellectual honesty the Roman position on the "pelvic issues" of birth control, the celibacy of priests, and the ordination of women.

Still another leave-taking occurred when I accepted a Fulbright

Fellowship and went to teach English in Yugoslavia for a year. This Communistic, atheistic, and extremely sexist country further challenged my spiritual identity. I lived in Skopje, Macedonia, a city surrounded by the Vodno Mountains. I frequently observed the mountain women with veiled faces walking three feet behind their men, an example of male domination that repelled me.

Male domination was also evident in daily sexual harassment. I was harassed by bus drivers, by businessmen in airplanes, and by colleagues. Men loitering in front of restaurants and cafes would recognize my American coat and shoes and shout out to me, "*Ah, Amerikanka, dodgi ovde!*" "Come here, American woman, come here!" By the time I returned to the United States, I felt not only alienated from myself, but betrayed as a father's daughter who had identified with the patriarchal system, a system based on the belief that man is superior to woman. I was not only hurt and disillusioned, I had become an angry woman.

What to do? A strategic solution: I returned to graduate school. My refuge now was studying counseling psychology. For the next ten years or more, psychology became my religion. My priest and confessor was a therapist who listened to me weep about my lost self and about how I felt betrayed and broken. My evangelists were my own experiences of fear, anger, sadness, and guilt. My scripture was the literature in psychology which described models of development rather than models of perfection. The greatest commandment was to discover who I was and to accept and love the self I was becoming.

My culminating leave-taking occurred in 1976 when I married Peter, a divorced Roman Catholic. In choosing him, I rejected the authority and tradition of the Roman church and of my parents. My parents expressed their disapproval not by direct anger or rejection but by hurt and disappointment. So now I was not only alienated from my deepest and most genuine self, I was also alienated from important communities. I was now a disobedient Father's Daughter.

What price did I pay? I believe it was a grave one. For the next fifteen years, I coped with a chronic illness, Crohn's disease, a serious inflammation of the lining of the digestive tract. I had only a few short periods of remission until surgery in October 1989.

Connected with my experience of coping with a chronic illness for fifteen years, however, is the realization that my suffering was not always pathological but transformative as well. In her book, *The Heroine's Journey*, Maureen Murdock describes a cycle of growth and maturity with which I can identify. She says that after being nurtured by the Good Mother as infants and young children, women learn to reject their feminine ground because it is devalued as weak or irrelevant and is feared in our culture by both men and women. We become Father's Daughters, seek approval and achieve success as defined by the patriarchal ego.[1]

At some point in our personal evolution, however, we come to a critical turning point at which we realize that we have no sense of self to call our own. We believe we have been betrayed, that we actually have betrayed our most authentic selves. We have become alienated from our own feminine ground. We become increasingly aware of the destructive and tyrannical Father who controls us from both inside and outside. We yearn for wholeness that requires redeeming the Terrible Mother buried deep within the Self. It takes tremendous courage to find her. For most, it means reclaiming our bodies, trusting our intuition, and acknowledging our need for an inner, female authority.

I can remember very well the most painful year of 1985. I was clinically depressed and experienced frequent periods of anxiety. For a number of months, I would wake up at 4:30 in the morning and read Sylvia Perera's *Descent to the Goddess*. She writes in the preface:

> We need to return to and redeem what the patriarchy has often seen only as a dangerous threat and called terrible mother, dragon, or witch. This inner connection is an initiation essential for most modern women in the Western world; without it we are not whole. The process requires both a sacrifice of our identity as spiritual daughters of the patriarchy and a descent into the spirit of the goddess, because so much of the power and passion of the feminine has been dormant in the underworld [the unconscious] and in exile for five thousand years.[2]

I identified with the Sumerian Goddess in the story who journeyed into the underworld, whose body was impaled upon a stake, who met her "Dark Sister," and in the end, was saved by something sacred, Holy Empathy. I believe my suffering became transformative, in part, because I received constant empathy and unconditional love from my partner, Peter, from my mother, and from my closest friends.

At the same time, I believe an essential part of my healing came from the experience of suffering itself. Nor Hall says in *The Moon and the Virgin* that "the healing of the feminine wound must be sought in the blood of the wound itself." I believe I entered into new depths of my Self, and in the end belonged more fully to the human community and, particularly, to the "community of the vulnerable."[3]

This vulnerability made me feel both weak and strong. I couldn't read about violence and left the room when television depicted violence. I was overwhelmed to hear that every six minutes a woman is raped in the United States, that every fifteen seconds a woman is beaten by her husband or partner, and that more than one-half of all American women will be victims of sexual assault or domestic violence in their lifetimes.

I searched for ways to connect with my alienated self. One summer, I covered my study wall with photographs. In the center, I placed photographs of myself at the ages of six months and ten, nineteen, and twenty-eight years. I needed to see myself every day. I included photographs of my family and, very important to me, of my great-grandfather, Franz, who was a weaver, and of my great-grandmother, Neza, a midwife.

I began to go to author and theologian Christin Lore Weber for spiritual direction. She helped me reclaim buried feelings and the voice of my intuition. She helped me discover and name an important Wisdom figure inside me whom I call the "Babushka Lady." She is the wise, Slavic, peasant woman in me, and the crone I am becoming.

I celebrated my fortieth birthday by inviting seven of my women friends to stay overnight, the way we did as adolescents. I created a ritual to celebrate myself and my relationship with each of them. I bought a large picture frame and made a collage of eighteen photographs of important women in my life. I told my birthday party guests who these women were and what gifts they had given me.

I entered the Master's program in theology at St. Catherine's. I saw it as an opportunity to come together primarily with women to study theology, Scripture, and the history of Christianity. No matter the course, what we did was help each other name our images of the Holy, honor what is feminine and what has been lost not only to ourselves but to the church and to the culture.

Perhaps one of the most significant connections I made during this important time of reclamation was consciously experiencing some kind of ineffable presence of my maternal grandmother, Louise Lokanc. I realized that, like the Presence of the Holy One, she had always been available to me. It occurred to me that for years, whenever I was feeling particularly vulnerable or inadequate, I would go to the piano and play a Slovenian song my grandmother had sung with such passion. I remember her singing it at the July honey picnics that the Slovenian priests and sisters held annually at the Franciscan monastery in Lemont, Illinois. I can still see Grandma even now; her matronly figure, dressed in one of her paisley dresses; her thick black hair pulled back in a bun, crowned with a navy blue straw hat with a few silk flowers on it; her crocheted handkerchief in hand and a purse hanging from her forearm. The song was addressed to Mary:

> Mother Mary, Mother Adored,
> The angel-spirits are singing to celebrate you.
> You call yourself Virgin,
> And you surrender yourself to the Word.
> Mother, be with me.
> Let this happen to me.

Adrienne Rich writes, "The woman I needed to call my mother was silenced before I was born."[4] Singing this song is a way of connecting with those sounds that connect me with the Mother in my Self.

These stories of my significant relationships and critical leave-takings reflect my own incarnation, dying and rising. The choices I made in separating from that which identified me primarily as a father's daughter and discovering the image of the Holy One in the Babushka Lady were moments of holy transformation.

Last Christmas a friend gave me a dumbek, a brass drum with a goatskin head. My Babushka Lady is telling me to make dumbek sounds, to connect with the rhythm, with the "I am" inside me, and to listen to where I must next take myself.

1. Maureen Murdock, *The Heroine's Journey: Women's Quest for Wholeness* (Boston: Shambhala Press, 1990).

2. Sylvia Brinton Perara, *Descent to the Goddess: A Way of Initiation for Women* (Toronto: Inner City Books, 1981).

3. Nor Hall, *The Moon and the Virgin* (New York: Harper & Row, 1980), 11.

4. As quoted in Perara, 13.

Reclaiming Native
American Symbols

Elona Street-Stewart

Shekinah, my oldest child, is a teenager. Her coming of age may be defined in many ways, including her prerogative to select the dress patterns I use when making her clothes. Her desires have made for some trying moments in the fabric store. Since she is the one to wear an outfit, she wants it to be "just right" for her, and since I am the one to sew it, I want a pattern that is cheap and versatile and that comes in multiple sizes.

These requirements are all negotiable, and we are getting better at compromise as we go along. I feel I am getting somewhere: teaching her how to consider a variety of options and preferences and passing on my practical skills help her give shape to unseen desires. The most difficult part, though, is also the most significant. She looks at the pattern catalogs and the models, drawn by an artist or photographed, and substitutes herself. If she does not literally like the "mirrored" image, she balks at giving the pattern a second thought. All the descriptions and possibilities I offer are lost to her because she does not yet know how to look at those pictures and see a pattern separated into sections of the whole; she does not yet trust that the pattern can be traced onto a variety of fabrics, colors, textures, and grains. She bases her prejudiced consideration of the unknown outfit on what she has observed before her eyes, on the outfit already interpreted and drawn, as if making her choice from a rack of ready-made dresses.

We each have a role here, my daughter and I, talking and sharing in the fabric store, talking and sharing about culture. Who knows who is the expert? The significant role to acknowledge is that the current moment is set in a convergence of the reality of what is seen and a tailoring of pattern and meaning from the imagined. Just as when I share Native American myths and unique symbols, knowledge is being passed on from one of us to the other, so am I educating my daughter by passing on traditional knowledge, expecting her to wake up and try on her own truth.

This has been my experience as a Delaware Nanticoke. I have learned that truth is not a series of facts but a series of patterned observations colored by our imaginations. This is the power of myth. Long ago our name meant the "People-Who-Live-by-the-Water." We were among the first Indians to be displaced by the increasing settlements along the Atlantic shore. Our oral traditions relate stories of tree-destroying Finns, Dutch captains, Swedish builders, Moorish sailors. Such stories connect us to incidents that predate the English settlements along the shores of Virginia and Maryland, giving us common understanding through all the threads that are braided into our history. Thus we realize the power of the myth. My historical perspective is that I am familiar with more than one America.

Our name no longer means the People-Who-Live-by-the-Water. As a consequence of relocation and genocide, the name came to mean the "Mixed-People." Tribal identities were blurred and clan distinctions were discarded as others abandoned their homes and villages along the Delmarva Peninsula and joined my people. Today "Nanticoke" should mean the "Survivors" in testimony to the remnants of people who survived against immigration and obliteration. I come clothed and colored by the myths of my people. I know the awareness of being a conquered people. I see an embroidery of post-traumatic stress disorders upon the descendants of those aboriginal people who suffered catastrophic social trauma and cultural conquest. The American Myth labels this as the Plight of the American Indian: unemployment, drug and alcohol abuse, disease, suicide.

However, something incongruous exists between the reality of what is seen and the pattern of the imagined. When the fabric of the Indian community is reconstructed by a change of social image, the undesirable can be transformed from cost to contribution. In light of this, the American Myth also celebrates a holiday for the discovery of America, called Thanksgiving. At Thanksgiving time the Indians are recognized, fleetingly, for all they have contributed to America.

As a recipient of traditional knowledge, I have been led to discover my own truth in the meaning of all this. But I do not talk about Indian symbols and perceptions as something to be borrowed and tried on in the American Myth. Others cannot claim our cultural symbols. America cannot even claim our conquest as an accessory to its history.

Back to the storytelling in a fitting room where the current moment is set in a reflection of the order and meaning of the reality of Native American culture. I, as storyteller, will describe Native American symbols as part of our spiritual nourishment, and the listener is left to find and design her own truth.

There is no *one* Indian religion or image; there are many cultural and tribal differences. Yet in storytelling, certain themes and symbols commonly appear. In an autobiographical essay, Jimmie Durham, Cherokee writer, echoes these succinct words of a colleague: "In this century the story of any Indian is a typical story, no matter how different."[1] He means that whatever the pattern of our lives, we are still The People, sewn with the same stitches. We are always to recognize the pattern in everybody who is probably related to us. My dad used to look at someone and say, "Yes, he's different, just like us." As a "Survivor" I am aware of the possibility that being mixed-blood could make someone's daughter, my sister; that elder, my grandma; this brother, my uncle. They are the mirrors through which we imagine and discover our own truths.

Once a theologian asked me about spiritual material that might be collected as evidence of the Indian theology we had been discussing. What could I send him to increase his awareness of and resources for inclusive theology? He really believed I could offer him some material. Acting out of his American Myth, he assumed such a professional consideration would evoke a reciprocal response: "Oh, here, I'll just make up a list of all the books, videos and music and accumulate them for you." He assured me it all could be sent C.O.D. for my convenience and promptness. I endured his blind comments, while attempting to explain that the dimension of Indian spirituality that I had shared would not be available in the artifact form he presumed everyone had. I was thinking of the tastes and smells, the art and ceremonial pieces, the stories and humor so evident and familiar in people's homes. I especially thought of photographs. Photos form a commonality—in most Indian homes photos stuck in mirrors, taped on cupboard doors, framed on dresser tops, stashed in drawers. These pictures are the evidence of what the people hold as valuable: the sons and daughters, the dancers and servers, the singers and elders, the babies and hunters. Yellowed and dusty with age or Polaroid crisp and shiny, these photographs are displayed to tell the stories.

I remember a recent visit to the Fort Peck Reservation in Montana. Sitting in a modern, prefab project home, I was surrounded by traditional patterns: wooden racks of dried squash rings, pounded meat drying over the washing machine, beadwork and jewelry pinned on the walls, feather chests stacked behind the couch, jars of dried corn and chokecherry jelly in the cupboard, elk roasts wrapped in the freezer, and photographs everywhere. I glanced through one whole album reserved for photos of the memorial feast for the mother of the hostess. About a year after a funeral, a traditional memorial feast takes place in honor and remembrance of that person. The family dedicates the serving of the meal in the person's memory and distributes gifts to the invited guests. They make a ceremonial display of photos, clothes and personal items. Traditional dancing and worship take place.

In this case, the family shared with me how the daughters had gathered together to be with their mom as her health deteriorated. They gave a dinner and giveaway. Then after her death, they made plans for the memorial. My hostess, one of the older daughters, was a grandmom herself, working full-time at work and at home. Her husband, twice retired, was involved in many tribal and church activities. For a year they lived on simple meals, saving all their meat, vegetables, coffee, and food budget for the memorial dinner. The five daughters got together every night after work to sew quilts. Each took her place at the rack, four at the corners and the slowest sewer in the middle. Once the corners and sides were done, so would be the center section. In that year they handmade sixty-four star quilts, eighteen star quilt pillows, and many shawls and ribbon shirts. They also collected and prepared traditional foods. Sons and daughters, relatives and friends, all came for the memorial. Hundreds of people were fed and received these lovingly made gifts.

All of this is testimony to the spiritual dimensions of that home. From the terminal diagnosis, to the death, to the memorial event—all might have gone unnoticed by the trained theologian. The depth and breadth of the giveaway material would have been unrecognized. Culturally significant values and items to share, events and persons, times and places woven together like quilt pieces—these would have gone as unnoticed as sewing basket remnants.

In the Indian tradition, the oral story, not written pages, presents history, relations, and experienced truth. Often the selection of experiences presented at the memorial provides survival material for the people and their future. The images and symbols are important because they measure out essential values for the listener to discover. Storytelling reclaims the cultural patterns so listeners can piece together historical and future moments. Great freedom exists in relationships among people, family, medicine, power, nature, and magic. There is also a great freedom between moments in time. Sequence is not necessarily chronological. Facts are not the design; they are subordinate to essential truths of life. Everything is connected to the land, the people, and their survival. Place names, events, and feelings carry meaning. Each part is whole unto itself and can be rearranged and reclaimed in a convergence of events, time, and space. For us, truth and memory are instinctive. Sometimes we display our symbols proudly. Sometimes we try to camouflage them. Yet, like family relations, they are always acknowledged.

A few years ago, sitting around the wood stove in a room barely furnished and reflecting the habits of the medically-disabled elderly, I was with a group that received a rich, intimate, startling gift of life. Out on this South Dakota reservation, we were visiting about church business. The auntie chatted with us for a while, probably giving herself time to figure out who we were, and then she began telling us of the history of her people. We had not requested this as we had only talked about car distances and meeting times. Yet she recited the history of the cruel relocation journey of her people. How they were chased by soldiers three times about one hundred years ago. How people starved or froze to death. How soldiers had even tied ropes to the children's fingers, so that, when the young ones straggled behind on juvenile legs, they could be pulled along. She told how a man from Washington had come out and rebuked the soldiers and their captain for treating the people so hideously. She recounted how he had told the soldiers to pack up and made plans to close the fort, permanently. The people again were moved, this time to their present location. Then she went on to tell us about where each of her kids was, pointing to the photos on the walls. On into the second hour of her stories, we learned about the different missionaries who came to live with the people, the good ones and bad.

As we left, I discovered the thread of meaning in this moment—that the stories of Indian people always are selections of tribal history (and cultural conflict), family, religion/church. Each time the story is told, the fabric and patterns can be rearranged in that freedom of sequence, relationships, and occasion mentioned earlier. Each time the material is reclaimed as the Indian storyteller selects the order of events and symbols, including or omitting detail. The essential truth is what one needs to see.

Often in the American Myth, order and truth must grow out of chronology and individual struggles and achievement. Non-Indians grow tired of hearing our stories repeating what happened centuries ago, woven into the realities of our contemporary lives. Yet each of our struggles is a part of our shared past and our future as a people. And we know that we are up against an opposing standard by which our image is fashioned. We have been seen only as museum pieces, anthropological specimens, or historical markers, but not as visible people. Today, we still have to fight for our survival in the sports arenas, the courts, schools, churches, and museums. Because we have not assimilated, we are not yet seen.

Diane Glancy, a Cherokee poet and writer who teaches English at Macalester College, has written a poem that beautifully fashions the convergence of what is seen and what is imagined. In "Solar Eclipse" the storyteller awakens invisible and proceeds to sew on her identity until she becomes visible.[2] The design of the skirts and shawls is familiar, layers of relationships, events, feelings. The instinctive marks of memory and truth put a hole in place of a heart, and attach a hand to hold pain. Yet in this moment the hands of the storyteller create a story that reclaims all the giveaway material for the listener, tailoring a pattern and meaning from the imagined. A story like this is for anyone who needs to discover the essential truth.

1. Jimmie Durham, "Those Dead Guys for a Hundred Years," in *I Tell You Now*, eds. Brian Swann and Arnold Krupat (Lincoln: University of Nebraska Press, 1987), 158.
2. Diane Glancy, "Solar Eclipse," in *I Tell You Now*, eds. Brian Swann and Arnold Krupat (Lincoln: University of Nebraska Press, 1987).

5.

Language:
Binding and Freeing

I would hope that the hierarchy could recognize another magisterium—where men and women are allowed to preside in church, to exchange the language and revise the readings, to celebrate women's experience as exquisitely valuable and sacred.

RAE GARDNER
Theological Insights, October 2, 1987

Bound to Freedom

Lyn Miller

Language is a great mystery, paradoxical at its core. It is all we have to know and to tell the truth, and yet what gives it its distinctive, powerful character is its capacity to lie. Words represent for us what is; they make the world present to us and us to the world. When we name something, we call it forth, give it discrete being out of the chaotic sea of our senses. What we put into words becomes real and binding for us.

While words can represent what is, they can also misrepresent which is both curse and blessing. This power to misrepresent has meant for women power to rob us of ourselves, of one another, of nature, and of God, of the ground on which we stand, the redemption that is coherence. Conversely, as the power to represent what is not, this chimeric character of language gives us poetry and fiction, dreams, fantasies, memory, and vision, the capacity to imagine a renewed heaven and earth. So the wanton character of language both destroys us and saves us. It grants us a world fixed yet always open to change by changing our words.

My own story has been generated by this paradoxical nature of language. The primary words that have woven my life are the words of the Bible, the words of poets, and the dark trinity of words hurled at me in my high school years: queer, lez, homo.

The world of the Bible, in my childhood, was a world not only

74

of words but of body. It was the physical world of the evangelical Lutheran church in which I heard proclaimed the elegant and opaque phrases of the King James version. The words themselves were physical; incomprehensible but protective talismans. God, back then, was a place: the shadowy, damp basement of the Sunday School; the huge, metallic church kitchen where early on Saturday mornings Ivan, the janitor, sipped his scorched coffee; the gym, which reeked of sweat and mildew and rotten tennis shoes. And God was Mrs. Edstrom, the choirmother, who exuded Emeraude perfume, painted her lips bright red, and whose spike heels punctuated her presence on hollow tiles. God was a patch of sun-splashed lilies of the valley that shivered in the high, narrow window, the thunder of the organ, and the earnest and fierce cadences of Pastor Peterson preaching hellfire.

Perhaps, most of all, God was the deserted balcony of the sanctuary on Saturday afternoons, where I stretched out in the space and silence, in the presence of a God who searched me and knew me from the womb, who loved me with an everlasting love from which neither angels nor principalities could separate me. In that virginal shelter where for a few hours I was neither daughter nor sister nor even girl, but free as God, I wrote my first poems.

But the Bible was not my only text. I was crazy for the poetry of Wordsworth, Dickinson, and Emerson. Their work celebrated the natural world in which I took so much pleasure, celebrated the exhilarating liberty of the individual and the sanctity of the heated emotions that thrilled through me. Poetry affirmed my worldly desires and dreams, was a reply to the self-abnegation and world-abnegation purveyed to me as biblical mandates. I believed in the Bible, but I believed in the poet's world, too. The poets led me to believe that I did not have to renounce myself to be a religious person.

These worlds made of words were my sustaining truths. But they were shattered by other words, false words but potent and devastating. When I was fifteen, in 1965, I made my first real friend and fell completely in love with her. She was someone I chose, and who chose me, to whom I could pour out all my passions and memories and hopes, and from whom I received the same back. It was as if I had entered a new world order, as if a door had opened in my ordinary days through which heat and glory poured. I wrote out my passion in love poems that sounded all-too-suspiciously like Dickinson, Elizabeth Barrett Browning, John Donne, Tennyson's elegy to H.H.H. And these poems fell into the hands of my teenage brothers and their buddies, who were embroiled in their own adolescent deformation into patriarchal manhood. After that, the words homo, lez, and queer became a litany. The language of shame and ostracism, these became the words by which all other words in the world were judged.

I used to walk up and down the streets trying out their sounds. *Homo.* It sounded to me like homely, whore, horrible, hobo. *Homo sapiens,* I thought. A name for being human. How did it become an insult? And was not every *Homo sapiens* also a *homo sexualis? Lez* was even worse. It sounded to me like "lizard," something scaly, slimy, mottled green, with beady eyes and a darting tongue; something that lived under a rock with the sole purpose of emerging to terrify people. Could this be me? Eventually I settled for *queer.* "Queer" was a word not much used by Americans. I could hear it on the lips of an elderly, dowdy, yet fastidious British spinster, sipping tea and wondering about her unusual neighbor. It suggested something eccentric but basically harmless, something quaint, slightly occult, a source of puzzlement more than consternation.

These words—homo, lez, queer—became for me like the scarlet letter on Hester Prynne's bosom. There was a silence surrounding them deep as a starless night that echoed back through the fathoms of space forever. My trust in the world that had created and nurtured me was completely shattered by these words and so, apparently, was its trust in me. I had failed, quite in spite of myself, to become the right kind of person, of woman. One day I was a prim and pious evangelical Lutheran, a slavishly adoring father's daughter, and the next day, according to my Dad, I was a slut and a pervert. I was out at the edge by myself. Had anyone else ever been there? Had anyone else ever loved her friend enough to want to marry her? Where were the poets now when I needed them?

At that point, instinctively, I began to keep a journal. Evidence was critical. I needed a witness, even if an imaginary one.

Eventually I did find evidence of others like me. I found it in so-called dirty books, in medical case studies of deviance, in criminal annals, in biblical proscriptions, in pornography. I tried hard to fit this degrading taxonomy onto myself, to accept that this was what I was—criminal, perverted, abominable, pornographic. I tried to burn it into me, partly, I think, because it was better than being nothing, better than to have no words at all to make me real, to give me social reality.

But I fought back, too, thanks to the poet's trust in experience. I searched through the Bible for references to homosexuality and then compared a great number of translations, some of which called us homosexuals, some perverts, and some homosexual perverts. Finally, with some relief, I concluded that there were homosexuals who were perverts and homosexuals who weren't, and God was upset only with the perverted ones. I also searched for countertexts. "Nothing is unclean in itself," Paul wrote, "but it is unclean for the one who thinks it is." And "If I speak in the tongues of men and of angels, but have not love, I am as sounding brass or a tinkling cymbal." And "Do not let what is good to you be spoken of as evil." "Whatever you do, do it to the glory of God." I wanted to love Denise to the glory of God because I felt God had given her to me. I trusted the praise in my body and soul.

And I admit I trusted God. I was convinced, and still am, that a God who made me as I was and called me to love as I loved and gave me the incredible gift of my friend, and then repudiated his work and his gifts, could not be God; and even if he were God, human beings were capable of greater compassion than he, and I would have nothing to do with him, even should he strike me dead. I was in good company there with Emily Dickinson, who prayed of her love for Susan, "Whatever Realm I forfeit, Lord, / Continue me in this!"; and with Ivan Karamazov, too, who refused a salvation predicated on the destruction of the innocent. I decided that if I had to choose between what the Bible said about God, and what I knew about God, I would choose what I knew.

But God was one thing and the church another. The church tore me from that blissful web where word and flesh once were one. I was to serve the word, and the flesh be damned. I was to subdue body and cling to spirit. I was to extract God from that web and forsake basketball, sweat, lilies-of-the-valley, Mrs. Edstrom. The letter of the law prevailed over life. I had the Bible thrown at me as a weapon. This I would not accept, so I left the church.

But none of my bravado could spare me from the emotional loss of my family and eventually of my friend, who couldn't bear the pressure on us, and who wanted more than anything to be normal. The loss of my family was particularly hard because it was never acknowledged; it became part of the tormenting, resonant silence as we went on eating and watching TV and brushing our teeth together while my heart was broken. I learned to stop love and desire in myself, to separate from my body, because that was my only hope of purity and worth, my only hope of endurance.

After four or five years of this, I reached the point where I was prepared to sacrifice everything I had been, known, and loved, if necessary, to make love to a woman. Part of the courage for this came from the death of my oldest brother in the service. My body came back to life to fight against death. I needed to live for his sake, if not my own, because he couldn't. So I "came out."

"Coming out" is an expression in the gay community for naming oneself and thus calling oneself fully into being. This expression communicates something of the self-split that most gay people experience between our natural feelings and our socialization. It is an ironic version of the debutante's coming out, in which what has been forming into maturity is presented to the world. First, we come out to ourselves; we name to ourselves what we, in fact, feel and want and dream, and perhaps have done but have denied. Then we tell someone else, with words or lovemaking, because we also need hearing; we need to be received and authenticated.

What made it possible for me and most other gay people to come out was the Stonewall riots of June 1969. Throughout most of history, at least Christian history, being gay has been a crime, and terrible punishments have befallen homosexual people, including torture, imprisonment, the death penalty, and Nazi concentration camps. Gay bars in the United States had long been raided by vice squad officers who rounded up bands of lovers and hauled them to jail just for being discovered in a gay bar. Finally, one hot night on Christopher Street in New York, gay patrons at the Stonewall Bar resisted the incursion of the vice squad into their private domain with what turned into three days of violence and torching. That was the beginning of the gay liberation movement in the United States. It ignited a new story of dignity, self-determination, and open, political community.

In the fall after Stonewall, while a student at the University of Minnesota, I noticed an ad in the school newspaper announcing a picnic for gay people at Riverside Park. I will never forget the impact of that ad. It was monumental, thrilling, unnerving evidence, which I snipped out and carried in my pocket. I pondered the word *gay*. I knew I didn't feel very gay, in the customary sense of the term, about my identity, though soon that word would develop the associations of flamboyance, audacity, color, élan, liberty. In the beginning I took it for euphemism, and for optimism.

As it turned out, I did not attend a picnic, but rather a dance at Coffman Union at the university. In the smokey, sweltering basement, dozens of shadowy figures became familiar with one another's faces, voices, smells, moves. We exchanged only first names, and those names were often not true. Gathered in the free zone of the dance floor, we were people who had bled from the woodwork, all our stories of silence and erasure, of ridicule and rejection, different in detail, and yet the same. We were being born into a new family, the family of each other. As the Bible birthed the world of the church for me, so "queer," "lez," "homo" birthed this world; a new nation behind unmarked doors, in pockets of night, or in private homes behind whitewashed façades with neighborly, flowering trellises. We closed that momentous evening whirling hand in hand in a great circle, weaving like a lithe, black, powerful snake among the pillars, singing, "Let the sun shine, let the sun shine, let the sun shine in."

I came out during the closing days of the reign of the bar culture, which lost its hegemony to our new daylight existence. At that time, women still played butch and femme roles. My new lover told me I was a butch, took me to a men's clothing store and dressed me in linen, silk, and leather; she changed my name to Donné, which she spelled like the French word for "give." The world of the bar was a world created by the rhetoric of curse and epithet. From the street, gay bars were unrecognizable. They had no marquee. Their entrances were unlit. They were known by word-of-mouth. Inside, one entered a theater of *amor fati*, the elegant, shameless, exuberant defiance of our fate. We were criminals. We were outlaws. It was a crime to be what we were, to touch one another as we did, a crime to walk down the street dressed in the clothes of the opposite sex. The bar could be raided at any time. *Amor fami* arose from this imputed criminality. A people born into crime despite themselves are bound, for their own dignity, to turn their fate ironically into their triumph, their trademark. We made the labels our own with high style, with the reckless vibrancy of being outside the law.

Within a couple of weeks of coming out, I was deeply branded by this "imputed criminality." I was forbidden by my father to go home again or to have anything to do with my younger brother and sister. I was asked by the women's boarding house on campus where I lived to vacate my room. I was dismissed from my job in a hospital because I refused to see a psychiatrist. I looked in the mirror and saw an unfamiliar person named Donné, a fledgling desperado. I had lost my family, my history, my cherished haunts, my livelihood, my expected future, absolutely everything I had been and everything I knew.

The result of this for me was a total deconstruction of the self into which I had started out. Nothing I had been told in my growing up had prepared me for the way my life was turning out. I could not sustain so much shock and loss. After a few months I signed myself into a psychiatric ward where my therapist took up the practice of calling me Donné-Lyn, the hyphen acting as a suture between my new self and my abandoned self. I had progressed from "criminal" and "tramp" to "sicko."

My experience in the hospital transformed me. But what was wrong with my treatment was its interpretation of the problem. It regarded what happened to me as a function of my own disturbed psyche. I was not strong enough to bear my pain. I was what had to be changed, not the world. My therapists never asked the larger question of why? Why did not only I but thousands and thousands of other human beings lose their families, their homes, their work, their history, their hope, even their very lives, in times past (and in times to come?), for taking in their arms lovingly a member of their own sex? Why does this matter so much to so many, causing mother and father to drive from the house children they had welcomed, known, and loved?

The answer to this is that it is easier for patriarchy to deconstruct me and others like me than to deconstruct itself. And that's what's at stake. Homosexuality violates the social and political order, which patriarchy would like us to believe is the order of nature. It is intrinsically a dissent from the power relations we have long taken for granted, power relations based on gender, on the hegemony of God over creation and man over woman and word over flesh. It walks away from these power relations, these property relations. Male homosexuality in particular draws to the surface and makes us notice that patriarchy itself is homocentric, is a world made by men, for men, in which their bonds with one another are primary. It is important that not too much attention be paid to the fact of this institutionalized eros because, if it becomes self-conscious, it undoes itself from within. Its peculiar male-to-male purity is exposed and disrupted. Do we not see this homoerotic order expressed in the traditional image of the Trinity as Father, Son, and Spirit, contemplating its self-complete masculine oneness? Homophobia—the persecution and suppression of homosexuals—functions to mask the contempt for women the male order wants to hide. Once these power relations become explicit, they cry out for change. Thus simply for women to begin calling the Holy Spirit feminine destabilizes the old order.

All of us at the margin, whether gay, black, Indian, Asian, disabled, poor, or simply female, understand how the deceptive ideological rhetoric of patriarchy puts the onus on us individually, or as minority groups, in order to preserve its system of privilege. And so we learn to embrace our marginality actively, to use it to become prophets; we learn to renounce inherited language and imagery, to invent our own, or to turn the inherited language back on itself in ironic and original ways, so that it becomes its own undoing.

This happened for me. The Christian story that damned me, saved me. When I came out of the hospital, I lived for a while in that liminal, miraculous, visionary place that one who has lost her self can enter. Religious traditions of every kind talk about this stripping-down, this dissolution of what stands between self and world. Our self is built of language, of the story we tell ourselves about how we arrived at the present, and the impetus the plot of that story gives to our actions and experiences in the future. Without a story, we are nothing but the moment's chaos of impressions.

Rationally, I lost my narrative thread. The story I told myself could not have led me where I found myself. Nor could the new story of my lesbian life in the bar culture avoid erasing everything that had gone before. But in that narrative gap, I existed in a flow of impressions that filled me with breathtaking, ecstatic liberty. I felt my embeddedness in nature and the human community at the most instinctual level. I knew I was not, and never could be, alone.

I realized that none of the words I had for anything were true—that is, ultimate—not the words for God, or for nature, or for the black neighbor children, not the words for myself given me either by the straight or gay culture. Words were absolutely vital, absolutely powerful, and yet absolutely empty. The mystery of self and world, while it must be spoken to be appropriated, to be endured, was nevertheless ultimately unspeakable. Everything was made up, thrown together, out of wind. I was born into *poesis*, or poetry-making, into the extemporaneousness of everything natural and cultural. I was born into a playful universe, calling itself into being by rubbing together the sticks of language, and then blowing out the fire and kindling it again. I was born into a language that bound me to freedom.

Out of this freedom, I was able to return to the riches of the Christian story without being trapped by them. I realized that I had lived what Jesus had talked about. I had lost my self to gain it. I had been destroyed for my unique vocation to love; I had descended into hell, and I had been brought back to life. I had been brought back to life because I believed, through my Christian training, that resurrection was the last word, that reconcilation was the last word, that justice was the last word, and that the one who endured to the end in that faith would be saved.

So, though Christianity is the child of patriarchy, I believe it contains in itself the seeds of the death of the tyrannical patriarch and the birth of a new, egalitarian world. But to usher it in, we must forbid the divine word to harden into the idolatry of dogma, of literalism, of essentialism about what it means to be man, woman, straight, gay, god, human, sacred, profane. When word takes up flesh, it must do so as theophany, not idolatry. For a little while, in the flash of the fire, we see in this word or that, the face of God, a light that illumines our path. We want to use these words as long as they shed light; they are all we have for light, but, when they stop being incandescent, we must let them go. Then the word-become-flesh is for us a living God, a still- and ever-creative God, not a graven image.

This transition into *poesis* implies an end to the hegemony of word over flesh. The word must serve the world, and not the world, the word. When the world is subjected to the word, it becomes the kind of world we now have, a world that betrays the flesh, the body, at every turn. By the body, I mean not only the personal human body, but also the collective human body, the social body, and the body of the phys- ical earth, the matrix in which we ultimately live and move and have our being. We all confront the realities of rape, incest, drug abuse, racism, hunger, poverty, war, gay-bashing, battering, and the con- tamination of our environment. These realities call into question every word that is spoken. Every word is answerable to these realities. What happens in the flesh has the last word. We can't trust words because they are in themselves made up, so we must judge them by their fruit, which is the world they make.

The Bible says that God died into the human; the divine Word emptied itself into the flesh even unto death. This means that the body is made holy, the body becomes divine speech. If we don't listen to the body, we can't know God. There is no other path. And that path is, as it was for Jesus, the path of passion, of reckless and total love in the face of hatred and ignorance.

I would not have chosen the life that has been given me. I have wanted to be pre-eminently a woman of spirit, a daughter of the word, accommodating and unobtrusive; but all my life has unfolded on the side of a renegade body, first in trying to renounce her, and at last in urgently defending her, in casting my lot with her though the moun- tains should fall and the hills turn to dust. I've had to say every day, somehow, yes, I am a sexual person. Sexuality, eros, is the heart of life, without it I am nothing. Without it there is nothing for any of us. Lust, desire, is the root of our life and our liberty.

The reward is that I have received a God for which the word "God" can never be adequate. I have received a God who cannot die, who searches me and knows me and has loved me enough to grant me resurrection, not once but over and over. I have received a self who knows her fragility, and that her fragility is her indestructible strength. I have received a body that fiercely clings to its knowledge, its pleasures, its right to be and to be cared for; a body that, without shame, grasps the abundant breast of this earth. I have learned that Woman is holy, that to be her and to love her leads me to life and truth and power and transcendence. I have learned that power is at the margin, where all of us who have been pushed out gather slowly into a storm that readies to pour its hard, life-giving rain on this parched earth.

I don't mind being a homo. For freedom I have been set free, and this freedom is precious. I have turned the whore into a vestal virgin, a sacred prostitute, who gives of herself without giving herself away, who is never owned. I have settled peaceably into the occult life of an eccentric spinster. And I have found that a lot of interesting life goes on under the rocks where lizards dwell. Slime is fertile, and a darting tongue has many good uses, and when was there a prophet who did not terrify people?

Besides, the world has changed. I no longer have to search between the words of poems to find my own truth reflected. I don't have to read medical case studies. We now have extraordinary lesbian poets like Adrienne Rich, Audre Lorde, Olga Broumas, Marilyn Hacker, Joy Hargo, Judy Grahn, and Minnie Bruce Pratt, who write magnificently about the love of women in this still-harrowing world.

And I now have discovered Spirit of the Lakes Ecumenical Church, a primarily gay and lesbian community, where, in a large warehouse, hundreds of us gather weekly from many traditions to stand upright in the House of God and, out of the liberating stories of the Bible, make redeeming sense of our histories and passions.

Slowly and steadily, with them and the poets, I exorcise the lies that broke me, and craft a saving truth.

Static and Emerging Metaphors for Women

Ann Redmond

Amy Lowell in her poem, "Patterns," creates a metaphor in which the speaker compares the societal constrictions on women to the freedom of daffodils. "For my passion/Wars against the stiff brocade. The daffodils and squills/Flutter in the breeze/As they please."[1] Besides alerting my senses, the words of gifted poets can draw me into the heights and depths of human experience by grasping my mind and heart. Amy Lowell's word-power here lies in the creation of a figure of speech, a metaphor.

The power of metaphor goes far beyond figures of speech, however, into the language of our everyday lives. The metaphors of everyday language, often subtle or even hidden, reflect and shape values and attitudes in our society. The most powerful metaphors are concepts rather than figures of speech; they are the thoughts that underlie the words we hear or see. These underlying ideas are conceptual metaphors.

Let me describe a familiar advertisement. The woman's eyes are heavy with mascara, her lips painted purple. A deep blue satin turban and gown encase her head and body. The sultry seductress extends her snakeskin clothed arm to show a snake's head formed by the elongated meeting of her thumb and forefinger. In addition to giving the impression of a snake's head, her hand holds a black bottle of perfume called "Poison." This powerful ad continues the stereotype of woman as temptress, a metaphor reflective of Eve and the apple. Other ads, like those for perfume, for Calvin Klein Jeans, for many brands of make-up, and for a long list of other products, rely on this metaphor: *woman is temptress.*

Underlying metaphors like this have the power to shape and reflect values and attitudes and, in turn, can influence how we think and act. The metaphor, woman is temptress, concentrates on that narrow meaning, that stereotype, to the exclusion of other qualities of women. "Woman is temptress" is never printed in large letters in an ad. In the ad just described, verbally enhancing all the visual clues of color, position, and facial expression, except for the one word "Poison," is unnecessary. Advertisements for liquor, cars, and vacation trips through a seductive pose and an exposed body use negative images of women to sell products. Advertising in print, on radio, and on TV are powerful because underlying metaphors convey subtle meanings quickly and forcefully enough to bypass the analytical mind.

Advertising is not alone in furthering the metaphor of woman as temptress; both traditional and contemporary works of literature stereotype women in this way. Those stereotypes, grounded in conceptual metaphors, go far beyond the figures of speech mentioned earlier. Conceptual metaphors build a system or web of meanings much more powerful than an individual expression. Metaphors, both sexist and racist, have bound women of color into fixed stereotypes. For black and Mexican-American women in particular, writing that presents the image of the exotic, sexually uninhibited woman in her wildness and freedom from cultural norms, seduces the unsuspecting white male. In fact, until very recently, the only two literary images of Mexican-American women were the madonna and the whore. The dragon lady or the lotus blossom metaphor depicting the Asian woman casts her in no less a stereotypical role. Metaphors that become stereotypes are powerful because they influence thinking and attitudes and can even move beyond comparison to the equating of a person's life to the static confines of that existence.

Traditionally our culture stereotypes women as emotional and men as rational without questioning that stereotype or the value of the rational over the emotional. In *Metaphors We Live By*, George Lakoff, a linguist and cognitive psychologist, and Mark Johnson, a philosopher, note that, in their studies of language, the metaphors "rational is up" and "emotional is down" are prevalent. Such expressions as the following support their thesis:

The discussion fell to the emotional level, but he raised it to the rational level.

She couldn't rise above her emotions.

He stood there like a man and didn't break into tears.

We put our feelings aside and had a rational discussion of the issue.

Whether or not we agree with all these metaphors does not alter the fact that they influence our lives. "Rational is up," "emotional is down," "time is money," "love is war," and other prevalent conceptual metaphors, on one level are clichés (dead metaphors); and we do not expect to find them in well-written literature, but what we may find in advertising and other writing will be expressions for these underlying metaphors. The danger of these "dead metaphors" lies in the fact that they are actually alive but subtle. Readers and listeners can identify powerful underlying metaphors by examining the subtle meanings underneath expressions.

George Lakoff and Mark Johnson along with Mark Turner, a literary critic, have developed methods for identifying and categorizing conceptual metaphors, such as those just mentioned. In addition to his work in the previously mentioned *Metaphors We Live By*, Lakoff collaborated with Mark Turner in *More Than Cool Reason: The Field of Poetic Metaphor*. In both of these works, the authors' findings show that one reason for the power of conceptual metaphors is that they form a system of interrelated meanings. These authors show specific examples of everyday expressions that, when viewed within a system of relationships, demonstrate powerful conceptual metaphors. The existence of conceptual metaphors underlying common expressions reveal undeniable values and attitudes within our culture, embodying much greater power than the linguistic expressions we know as figurative language.

Evidence of such a system of interrelated meanings is shown in a study that George Lakoff did with Zoltan Kovecses and which Lakoff reported in *Women, Fire, and Dangerous Things*. Their study shows the similarity of expressions and metaphors describing both lust and anger. They record uses of language that voice underlying attitudes and values substantiating the existence of the conceptual metaphors such as "woman is sexual object," "woman is her body," "woman is victim," "woman is temptress."

Their research shows that anger and lust are clearly emotions for which our culture generates abundant language. The central and most generally accepted metaphor for our understanding of anger is "anger is heat," and many expressions describing lust echo that conceptual metaphor. I have selected some of the expressions recorded by Lakoff and Kovecses in their study.

ANGER IS HEAT:
Don't get hot under the collar. They were having a heated argument. You make my blood boil. He blew a gasket.

ANGER IS INSANITY:
She went into an insane rage. You're driving me nuts. He got so angry, he went out of his mind. When my mother finds out, she'll have a fit.

ANGER IS AN OPPONENT:
You need to subdue your anger. He lost control over his anger. She fought back her anger.

ANGER IS A DANGEROUS ANIMAL:
He has a monstrous temper. He unleashed his anger. He has a fierce temper.[2]

Lakoff infers from the study that relationships exist between the metaphors for anger and the high incidence of rape in our country. In some cultures, rape is virtually unknown, but this study suggests that the way we conceptualize both lust and anger, together with our various folk theories of sexuality, may be a contributing factor to many instances of violence against women.[3] Expressions about lust make this connection explicit.

LUST IS HEAT and related expressions are similar to ANGER IS HEAT. She's an old flame. I'm burning with desire. He was consumed by desire. He's still carrying a torch for her.

LUST IS INSANITY. (ANGER IS INSANITY.)
I'm crazy about her. I'm madly in love with him. You're driving me insane. I'm wild over her.

LUST IS WAR. (ANGER IS AN OPPONENT.)
He's known for his conquests. Better put on my war paint. He fled from her advances. She surrendered to him.

LUST OUT OF CONTROL IS AN ANIMAL. (ANGER IS A DANGEROUS ANIMAL.)
He's a wolf. He looks like he's ready to pounce. He preys upon unsuspecting women. You bring out the beast in me.[4]

The metaphorical concepts underlying all of these expressions show the connections in our culture between lust and physical force, even war. Because of the language similarities between expressions for anger and lust, we can conclude that there must be links in our thinking between anger and lust. Just as one can have smoldering sexuality, one can have smoldering anger. One can be consumed with lust and consumed with anger. One can be insane with lust and insane with anger. Desire as well as anger can get out of control. The connection between the conception of lust and the conception of anger is by no means accidental. Such a connection has important social consequences as Lakoff suggests in *Women, Fire, And Dangerous Things.*[5]

Women's groups fighting pornography and exploitive language against women see these connections. Many examples in the language of advertising, both verbal and nonverbal, show anger and violence toward women. Often they are subtle, but the messages are there, messages of women being passive victims to be preyed upon, being sex objects, being temptresses and thus deserving of punishment. Readers and viewers often do not take time to analyze ads that illustrate anger and violence against women, but when attuned to exploitive language, they do not have to look far to find examples. Of course, ads that exploit men as macho role models provide another perspective on the same issue of stereotyping.

On the other hand, metaphors can present strong, positive images of women. More and more women writers in their poetry, novels, research writing, and essays generate new metaphors. They invite readers to hear and use language that truthfully reflects essential meanings of women's lives and attempts to counteract the effects of exploitive language.

One such writer, Suzanne Kobasa, in her doctoral research at the University of Chicago, calls for reflection on a strong metaphor for today's woman: "woman is hardy." In her dissertation, Kobasa describes differences between the woman who sees herself as a victim and the woman who possesses the characteristics of hardiness.[6] The victim views herself as having no choices after a traumatic experience, sees herself as not mattering, and sees no sense in being creative while assuming a victim identity. The woman who possesses hardiness has developed different characteristics: she has a sense that she is in control of her life; she sees changes in her life as challenges, not threats; and she has a sense of commitment to herself. She believes she is worthwhile and can commit herself to actions that are valuable. The use of the word, "hardy," is interesting. While it connotes strength, good health, and ability to cope, it never connotes the kind of strength that dominates another. Karen Hilgers, in her doctoral study (University of Minnesota) on hardiness and trauma levels, shows that, not surprisingly, the victim of rape who possesses hardiness is much better able to cope with the psychological trauma of rape.

Another metaphor, "woman is a builder of networks," underlies many of the endeavors engaging women's time and attention: creation of the AIDS Quilt, the art of Judy Chicago and her collaborators in "The Birth Project," Mothers Against Drunk Driving, Women Against Military Madness, and the many peace organizations in which women are a driving force.

Janice Raymond in her book, A Passion for Friends, identifies another positive metaphor to which today's woman can relate: "woman is thoughtfulness." To think of a woman as embodying thoughtfulness is certainly nothing new. Women are expected to be thoughtful; they have played that role for generations. Raymond suggests two ways to explain the word, "thoughtfulness": the ability to reason and the ability to be considerate and caring. She contends that this thoughtfulness should not be a compulsion or an indiscriminate giving to others that knows no limits. Women have been socialized to react almost instinctively to the needs of others rather than act out of self-directed thinking. That kind of thoughtfulness is actually the opposite of being full of thought.[7]

According to Raymond, thoughtfulness informed by thinking is necessary to the sustaining of friendship. Thinking is essential for persons to know and to dialogue with themselves; without that personal dialogue, they cannot communicate with others.[8] The metaphor, "woman is thoughtfulness," at its best brings together the two meanings of thoughtfulness described by Raymond and joins actions with thought.

Language-sensitive people, through their writing, speaking, and visual arts, can influence metaphors that present positive images of women: "woman is creator of networks," "woman is builder of relationships," "woman is a whole person—not just a body," "woman is hardy," "woman is a friend," and "woman is thoughtfulness."

Raymond and other writers present arguments persuading us to consider new metaphors for women, but novelists, too, persuade us through characters who triumph over seemingly impossible odds. Novelists of color, women who have been subjected to terrible violence and dehumanization, have created especially strong characters who triumph over adversity. Zora Neale Hurston's character, Janie, in Their Eyes Were Watching God, is one such example. Despite relationships with two men who try to rob her of all sense of self, she triumphs and becomes a strong woman. The novel is not about the terrible things that men do to women (although these things happen) but about the stereotypes that both men and women live out. The two men who most oppress Janie are themselves victims of society's stereotypes. In many ways Janie is a victim, but she clearly possesses the characteristic of hardiness, calling to the fore her own inner reserves despite dehumanizing experiences. She learns from and triumphs over her negative experiences. Her words at the end of the novel illustrate this:

> Here was peace. She pulled in her horizon like a great fish net. Pulled it from around the waist of the world and draped it over her shoulder. So much of life in its meshes! She called in her soul to come and see.[9]

Hurston, in showing a Janie who "called in her soul" (used all her life's experiences to become a strong, self-sufficient woman), makes concrete the conceptual metaphor: "woman is hardy."

Many women writers today are bringing new and life-giving insights to the everyday activities commonly ascribed to women: planting, cooking, cleaning. Helena Viramontes in her story, "Moths," describes the life-giving relationship that a rebellious granddaughter has with her wise grandmother.

> . . . I'd gladly go help Abuelita plant her wild lilies or jasmine or heliotrope or cilantro in red Hills Brothers coffee cans. Abuelita would wait for me at the top step of her porch holding a hammer and nail and empty coffee cans. And although we hardly spoke, hardly looked at each other as we worked over root transplants, I always felt her gray eye on me. It made me feel, in a strange sort of way, safe and guarded and not alone. Like God was supposed to make you feel.[10]

Viramonte's positive metaphor of the grandmother, a nurturer who reflects God, shows the life-giving power of a community of women.

In spite of the negative metaphors found in advertising, women writers are claiming new literary metaphors that can replace the negative stereotypes of women. Because these writers, as well as women and men from a variety of professions and lifestyles, are becoming attuned to the nuances of language and its power, there is hope. They are generating language to challenge and replace the stereotypes.

As Tom Stoppard says in his intriguing play illustrating the power of language, *The Real Thing*: "I don't think writers are sacred, but words are. They deserve respect. If you get the right ones, in the right order, you can nudge the world a little. . . ."[11]

1. Amy Lowell, "Patterns," in *By Women: An Anthology of Literature*, eds. Marcia M. Folsom and Linda H. Kirschner (Boston: Houghton Mifflin, 1976), 301.

2. George Lakoff, *Women, Fire, and Dangerous Things: What Categories Reveal about the Mind* (Chicago: University of Chicago Press, 1987), 382-392.

3. Ibid., 309.

4. Ibid., 410-11.

5. Ibid., 412.

6. Suzanne C. Kobasa, *Stress, Personality and Health: A Study of an Overlooked Possibility* (Chicago: University of Chicago Press, 1977).

7. Janice C. Raymond, *A Passion for Friends* (Boston: Beacon, 1986), 220.

8. Ibid., 218.

9. Zora Neale Hurston, *Their Eyes Were Watching God* (Urbana: University of Illinois, 1978), 286.

10. Helena Maria Viramontes, "The Moths," in *New Worlds of Literature*, eds. Jerome Beaty and J. Paul Hunter (New York: W. W. Norton, 1989), 1052.

11. Tom Stoppard, *The Real Thing* (Boston: Faber and Faber, 1984), 53.

6.

Living in Transition

Yearning for more is already a sign that the imagination of God is still alive in the people.

SHAWN MADIGAN, CSJ
Theological Insights, October 9, 1987

The Space Between

Sarah Hall Maney

Transitions straddle the fence—neither the cold of an ending, nor the heat and energy of a new beginning, but rather the lukewarm, the dull nothingness of in-between. Although we encounter and move through transitions at each stage of life, adolescence and middle age seem to be the times they crowd in on us in the most insistent ways. Physical, emotional, psychological, vocational and spiritual transitions all demand some attention.

The sound of the word "tranzzzzition" has, in my mind, always conjured up movement—something fast whizzing by—exhilaration—excitement—energy. Transitions seem to have three distinct parts: an ending of something (a role, a relationship, a vocation), a middle time (a neither-this-nor-that time when I have grieved the ending and wait for a new beginning that is not yet here), and, finally, some sort of reordering, a new beginning.

The middle time, that time of living in the space between an ending and a new beginning, is a period of time often overlooked or denied because, for many of us, it is messy and doesn't feel good. It has some suspicious characteristics that often appear unhealthy, regressive and certainly unproductive. In other words, the middle sections of transitions just don't fit the "American Way" of living!

When I grieve an ending, a loss, letting all my tears out, speaking of my anger, sadness, and confusion, I "hit the wall" of the middle time.

Then there are no more tears, no more sadness, no more anything; it is a time when I seem to be stuck at dead center. I don't so much miss the role or person or place that I have lost or left as I miss finding anything or anyone else very appealing, worth my time and attention. Depression and her sisters apathy, inertia, and negativity—often move in for a visit during middle times of transition.

Holy Saturday, the day that stands between Good Friday (the day of ending, loss, death) and Easter Sunday (the day of new beginnings and resurrection) is an apt metaphor for the middle time of transition. Let me share a prose poem, "Holy Saturday," from my 1982 collection, *Coloring Outside the Lines and Other Poems:*

And where are you now, asked the angel of God—Name your place!—she roared in my ear—the voice sounded like one of those "mind your elders" types, so I began to scurry around, looking for my "place." I knew for sure I wasn't living in the euphoria of Palm Sunday, although I remembered that lovely, sweet time, when I could reach out and touch Jesus and he leaned his head toward me every time I spoke or called—no, I had definitely left that place— Name your place! the angel said, so I hurried on to confront Good Friday. Ahh, the Good Fridays, they were certainly familiar, having been there so often and so lately—was I still living in Good Friday, with all the pain of letting go of the "olds" in my life, with the tears, fear, despair and wrenching of my heart? No, even though I could still feel the pains of Good Friday, I somehow knew I had walked on past, or perhaps I was carried on beyond Good Friday. Name your place! the angel blazed out—this was to be no "Sunday drive" of my mind—somehow I knew it was vitally important that I find that place where I live—so I rushed on to Easter Sunday—that Resurrection time; Oh, how I wanted to be there again—I remember the other times—the hope, turning to the joy that fills me, like the water rising on my body as I walk into the sea, rising 'til it covers my whole person and I am immersed and floating in the joy, and it is good. But try as I might, I just couldn't fit myself into the Resurrection place—Name your place! the command barked out—But I can't find it, I retorted. I've tried them all, and I don't fit anywhere—oh, how I hate being "no-where"—there's nobody else living in "no-where"—it's no place! You've missed your place, the angel shot back; you skipped over it, discounted it, disregarded and disdained it—Name your place!

And then I knew—Holy Saturday—that's my place! That's where I'm living now—yes, yes, I fit here—it is familiar—that dry, empty place where color leaves the eye, music leaves the air, salt leaves the food, import leaves the word, lilt leaves the step—and what is left, what is left? Does despair live here also—that black hole of nothingness that is so engulfing on the Good Fridays? No, thank God, I don't see despair living here in Holy Saturday—And what is here in its stead, to fill up its space? I don't know, I can't see it, I said. Yes, you can, the angel said—look more closely—and then, there in the corner, I spied her, sitting so quietly, yet with a certain dignity and strength about her—Hope sits there in the corner in place of black despair—She sits quietly, unobtrusively, because her thoughts are elsewhere—remembering the other Easter Sundays, the other Resurrection days—And you know, the most attractive, alluring quality about Hope is her patience—her optimistic patience—she accepts the process, the waiting, never taking her eyes off tomorrow, Resurrection Sunday. Holy Saturday is your place, the angel said. Yes, I know, I said, and joined Hope in the corner, relieved that at last, at last, I could stop the frantic pacing and sit down and rest.

The liturgies for Holy Saturday, at least in the Roman Catholic tradition, are taking on deeper significance. We have often regarded Holy Saturday simply as a day to rest from the drama of Good Friday and for the joy and jelly beans of Easter Sunday. I think we approach the middle time of transition in much the same way—often denying it even exists within us and in our lives. We want to skip directly from our endings to our new beginnings. Rather than live in the dreaded "in-between," we try to deny the ending by refusing to acknowledge that something has changed. We push ourselves on the ski slopes or tennis courts beyond our middle-age limits; we hang onto our college children with an overabundance of cards, letters, phone calls and care packages; we go the same places with the same people, saying the same things, smiling the same smile because to do otherwise would mean we would have to reexamine our whole life. We do not want to admit chaos and the terror of the unfamiliar. Some of us may not try to hold onto the past, but instead grab at anything that resembles a new beginning, paying no attention to whether or not we have any real interest in a new activity or relationship, only wanting to fill up our minds and our days with busyness. We can often see no particular virtue in sitting in the barrenness of the middle time.

But even though it may be so obscure as to be undiscernable, there is a reason for the "middle time"—the time between endings and beginnings, death and resurrection. I am reminded of the camp game we used to play, "Going on a Bear Hunt." As the leader would verbally bring the group to each obstacle, we all would chant, "Can't go under it, can't go over it, can't go around it, gotta go through it!" We too "gotta go through" our transitions. There is something of value in waiting for God to show us "what next," of not pushing the rhythm of our life faster than is natural, of hoping and believing that there is a pattern to our life even though we can't always see what it might be. Much of the middle time of transitions involves waiting. For the few or many of us who have temperaments that crave instant gratification, waiting for new beginnings to evolve can seem to be too much to ask, a task akin to watching grass grow. But waiting is integral to transition. I describe this process in another of my poems, *"Waiting"*:

How do I wait?
—like the old woman in her wheel chair?
folded, quiet hands, nodding head,
wrapped securely in her yesterdays
waiting, waiting so patiently, so silently
for her turn to die

How do I wait?
—like the florrid-faced man behind the wheel of his Lincoln?
—the motor races, his fingers drum and beat the wheel
he and the Lincoln, crouched, ready to leap forward
with an instant response to the blink of the light

How do I wait?
—like the restless, fretful child in the doctor's office?
a truck, a book, a cuddly bear—passing distractions
to be examined and discarded
His little body twists and turns,
looking for comfort and a restful position
Finally, in exasperation, he throws himself and his frustration
upon his mother's lap, to be soothed . . . and to wait.

How do I wait?
—like the tired, sagging woman in the grocery line
leaning behind the cart piled high with pizza and pop
hamburger and hot dogs
The woman is not really waiting in the grocery,
she is standing in line, waiting for her turn to live
Her eyes see not the reality around her, the homeliness of her life
No, her eyes see some distant illusion of youth, romance,
beauty, attention, and perhaps, yes, just possibly, fame
And so she waits for that day that never comes,
and throws away her todays
like pennies flung into a wishing well.

How do I wait?
Lord, I ask that you teach me how to wait
Teach me to wait patiently, yes
But more than that
teach me to wait creatively, joyously
Teach me to wait with my eyes on today
not looking back to my yesterdays,
nor forward to my illusions of tomorrow
Lord, teach me to wait.

For those women who have had children and have been full-time homemakers, one of the major mid-life transitions begins when our children become adults and are no longer a primary part of our lives. Our role as mother is significantly altered; our relationship with our husband shifts when we don't have the children as the central focus of our relationship and must look for new ways to fill our days. At last there is time to pursue our own interests, or return to school for more education, or move into a career that requires time and attention that we never had time to give to a job before. The middle time between the changing of our role and the beginning of something new that reflects our own self can be a confusing, lonely time. Often we have become so enmeshed in the lives of our family members that we don't know or remember what stimulates and enriches that deep-down core of our self. It may take some time to discover the core self which may have been lost amid children's piano lessons and hockey games, room mothering and den mothering, slumber parties and prom nights. We may venture out into some art classes or yoga, community activism or spiritual deepening, or a new job, only to find that one activity may give meaning and new depth to our life, another does not. Gone are the days of easy companionship with other women who were living lives similar to our own. We have lived lives of being someone's mother and someone's wife. So who is the real self, and will she please stand up? It is no wonder that this middle time of transition into self can be a confusing, lonely time. On the other hand, many women have been on the journey to self long before they encounter the empty nest. For women in other life styles, other changes may trigger the journey to self. None of us moves through a particular transition in exactly the same way in exactly the same time frame as someone else. It is important that we honor the unique qualities of our own and others' transitions.

Another common mid-life transition is one of moving away from being our parents' children, in order to parent our elderly parents. If our parents live into old age, the physical, emotional and psychological changes in them, may resemble a regression to childhood. Arthritis or other physical disease may make it difficult or impossible for a parent to open a jar, vacuum the floor, climb the stairs, drive the car. The diminished ability to see, hear and take care of one's self can alter the emotional stability of a once self-confident parent. Reduced mental capacity can be a further frustration. We, the children of elderly parents, can find ourselves caught in the middle, vainly trying to wear several hats at once. A part of us is still the child, wanting comfort, nurturing, reassurance from our parents. But our parents need the same thing from us, and so this "space between" is a time of finding the delicate balance.

Middle age is a "Holy Saturday" time of life. Our bodies and our mirrors tell us that we are no longer young, and yet we certainly don't think of ourselves as old—only other people get old. There are, however, disturbing signs. One morning I returned to the bathroom where my husband was shaving, admitting to him that I needed to brush my teeth, because I couldn't remember if I had already brushed or not. He looked at me blankly and said, "Well, if it helps you any to know, I can't remember whether you were in here before or not either." It is at least comforting to know we are growing old together.

Our culture does not help us much in making the transition between young and old. We know only too well the things we lose, what we give up as we age. But the opportunities we have in growing older—opportunities for wisdom, a better and larger life perspective, more self-knowledge, more competence and ability, are not as valued in our culture as the "youthful look." A beautiful young woman commands much more attention and admiration than a wise old woman. We read and hear about what a young woman, such as Brooke Shields, thinks and believes about life, but precious little of the wisdom of older women. Our culture seems to imply that as women age we have everything to lose and nothing to gain. As women, as sisters, we need to challenge and shatter this notion, by honoring one another's wisdom, by celebrating our aging, by sitting at the feet of our mothers and grandmothers so that we can listen to the stories, hear the wisdom, learn the lessons of life and, when it is our turn to be "the old one," have the courage to speak out and believe we have something of value to pass on to the young.

The physical changes in our women's bodies may be the most obvious signals of our aging. The time of menopause is a time of living in the space between young and old. Ironically, some of the manifestations of menopause are disturbingly reminiscent of adolescence. A woman living through menopause lamented her recent tendency to burst into tears in response to almost any emotion—joy, sadness, anger, tenderness. Does that remind us of our teenage daughters, whose tears could well up when we only asked if they had a nice day? For many of us, PMS is having one last monthly go-around within us before signing off. It is interesting that our bodies and emotions react in much the same way when our hormones are waning as when they are waxing.

Another transition that has been observed in middle-aged women is the transition from powerless to powerful. The dictionary defines power as "the ability to do—capacity to act—capability of performing or producing." If we age well, in accordance with God's plan for us to grow into our most whole and complete selves, we grow in knowledge, ability, wisdom. We received training and have lived experience. In reflecting upon who we are in this middle time, we know we have power—the ability to do and to act, the strength and capability to contribute and produce. So we know we are powerful; we have moved from powerlessness.

A new beginning involves finding ways and places to use this power. And for women to find ways and places to use our power effectively and authentically can be a difficult challenge. If we have been full-time homemakers, our wisdom and our power may be rich, but upon whom do we discharge it? Our children need and want to find their own ways of "making a home," and unsought advice is often labeled as "interfering." Many of us have grown in knowledge and wisdom and training through hundreds and hundreds of volunteer hours of community and/or church service. We know we have power in our chosen area, and yet when important decisions are made in a church or community setting, it is seldom the volunteer who is called in for advice and counsel. Sometimes, because power wants to be used, we misuse our power by dominating or lecturing, or controlling groups or individuals. It is sad when our power, so hard won, is diverted onto unhealthy, destructive, diminishing paths. For then we become stuck in this transition and never move on to the new beginnings.

Statistics reveal that, beginning in mid-life, significantly more women than men must face the transition from married to single when a spouse dies. Because the transition from the married to the single state (whether through death or divorce) involves so many other transitions, the movement from being married to being single may be the most difficult transition through which some of us are called to live. For not only must we cope with the loss of a partner, many of us must move to a new location, find new friends, learn new skills—in effect, find a new life.

One transition that is close to my heart seems to influence all my other transitions. I am aware of experiencing great transition in the area of my spirituality. My poem, "Holy Saturday," was written with my spiritual transition in mind. For spiritually I find myself in a nowhere place. I no longer find the church community to be "home" in the same way it once was. The liturgy and words of Scripture are not as often places to turn for insight or comfort or nourishment. My images of God have moved from Remote Being in the Sky, to loving Parent, to Friend, to Lover, to Mystery, to Absent One. It is a dark time, when the old rituals, traditions, and customs no longer fit or reflect my experience. I have hopes for new beginnings, but I do not yet know what they may be.

All women in transition, living in Holy Saturday, can remember that our friend Hope is with us. We can find her within us and around us, in our friends and neighbors. Let us be hope for one another, believing that the middle time is not the end—that for each transition there is a new beginning up ahead.

A Bridge of Faith

Rose Huntley

I delight in crystal because it is clear. I crave seeing clearly and always have. At eleven years of age, I donned glasses with relief, puzzled that friends and family felt sorry for me. I highly value my sight and insight. I like to be sure of matters by doing research before a major expense, investment, or trip. I value clarity.

What a shock, then, to find myself in a mental and emotional fog, with little clarity; the beginning of my conscious journey to wholeness began with disintegration and darkness.

When I was most separated from myself, God, and others, I was not aware of emptiness or darkness. I filled my life with a large busy family, teaching, and volunteer work in church and politics. But I experienced a void in my life when I began to let go of the stranglehold on those people and activities through which I defined myself and my worth.

Because my story impacts so many other lives, I have chosen not to share the details of deep separation in my life. However, I will share how I experienced the void through which I continue to seek connectedness.

I found myself in an in-between place where I realized that the old way was gone but was not sure what I wanted in the future. I stood basically alone in this liminal place. Support groups and friends exist for women like me, but they sustain, not undergird. When it seems as

102

though the foundations have been ripped out, those of us who experience the void feel lonely, desperate, raw, vulnerable, exposed. We may feel abandoned and a bit frantic. The old reasons do not work any more, and we cannot *make* them work. A friend, Mary Erickson, once said, "We experience the liminal place as total void, but through the power of faith we can interpret it as a bridge."

That spoke to my experience during a meditation image. Walking through a flat green landscape, I came to a great chasm blocking my way. I looked over the edge and saw the raw red soil and rocks descending into the earth and a wildly turbulent river cutting the abyss deeper. The cleft split the land as far as I could see on either side of me. Knowing my destination was not to the right or left, but straight ahead, I was terrified of the depth and the treacherous waters below. As I stared, wondering what to do, I saw a shadow move on my right and heard the hollow thud of something heavy landing on the ground. A huge wooden cross bridged the chasm. Clouds of red dust rose from the force of its landing. The cross looked smooth and worn, its patina glowing richly in the sunlight. That wood looked very narrow across the huge rip in the earth. There were no side rails; nothing on which to hang. Only that smooth worn wood stood between me and what I saw as certain death below. I had to choose. I was not sure of the purpose of this journey, but I did not want to remain on my side of the chasm.

I knew that to gain understanding, I would have to live into the meaning of this image. The idea of the cross was repugnant. At that time it symbolized the suffering and death I would have to experience to atone for my sinfulness. I did not feel love, only shame and responsibility. At the same time, an inner voice asked: "But what the hell did I do? What was so bloody awful that required the death of Jesus to satisfy God? What kind of blood lust does He have? What kind of God is that?" I did not want to pick up my cross and carry it; I had had enough already! I thought if I was willing to carry the cross, that capricious God would burden me with diseases or sorrows too heavy to bear. It seemed a dangerous venture to get too close to an angry God with such a wicked sense of humor. And yet, the only visible way across the chasm was the cross. Metaphorically, I struggled with the question, "Who is God?" for a long time before I could trust enough.

I experienced the loss of some beliefs I had previously accepted as true. I began to realize that some of my perceptions of life and people were not quite based on reality but upon a desperate attempt to control and protect my existence. My basic life questions were the same: Who am I? What am I doing here? Who is God? What is love? What are relationships for? Where am I going? Why? And how? Stale answers no longer satisfied me. Bedrock beliefs seemed to be blown away by circumstances beyond my control or understanding.

I recall a series of images I drew that illustrated this feeling. I was on a platform held aloft by four very tall stilts and surrounded by pink clouds of safety. Suddenly, one of the stilts broke, throwing the platform off balance. I said, "Oh, there goes one. It's okay, I have more." Then another support broke, and fell. "There goes another one . . . oh, no." Now I would have to move more carefully. When the third stilt broke and fell, I perched myself upon the one remaining supported corner and thought I could balance it. I told myself to hang on, just hang on. Meanwhile the pink clouds of safety had drifted off, and dark storm clouds surrounded me. I saw the last support begin to crack and bend. "Oh, no, it just can't. I'll fall and fall and never stop!" The stilt broke. I clung to the unsupported platform crying, "No . . . please . . . no—what will I do?" I fully expected to fall and be dashed on the rocks below. To my amazement, the platform floated. I did not understand. I was still there. I did not fall into a bottomless pit when the beliefs supporting me eroded. However, I felt empty, eventually realizing I would need to construct a solid foundation firmly grounded upon what *I* believe.

I found myself in a struggle to separate truth from lies. In this upside-down, liminal place, the meanings were lost. What was truth? I had imaged it as a banner in the sunlight, flying freely from a high standard. But some of the truths of my life have been horribly ugly and difficult to accept. I began to image these as an old hag in filthy rags coming to my door, smelly and inarticulate, wanting to step in and spend some time with me. This scrofulous old hag had a gift for me somewhere in the layers of her moldy garments, and the only way I could receive the gift of freedom was to invite her in, sit on the couch with her, and let the instruction begin.

I discovered the seeming ugliness of several truths and discerned the seductive beauty of some of the lies that kept me in bondage. The lies seemed beautiful because they were well worn and comfortable, like a favorite pair of shoes, and because I thought they were the truth. I believed lies about my lack of worth, beauty, inner goodness. I believed lies about my family of origin, about God, about the place of women in this world and in church structure. I do not want to impute motives here; those who taught me lies by their words or behaviors were probably lied to also. However, culpability is not the issue. Especially destructive to me were the lies that kept me unaware of my anger, my personal power, and a body truly wondrous and made in the image of God.

When we become aware that the people who modeled love, truth, and beauty for us are flawed, and that the God of our understanding is not adorable, to whom do we look? Where do we go? For a woman who had been carefully taught to doubt her own ability to discern truth, who had been encouraged to leave the job to older and wiser authorities, usually male, the journey toward truth and freedom has been both terrifying and exhilarating.

One of my mentors told me a Hasidic myth that gave me hope that I could discern truth. The Hasidim, a group of eighteenth-century Jewish mystics, believed that God infused the soul into an infant at the time of "quickening." At that time, Michael the Archangel was sent to bring the tiny one to the Creator, who found the baby adorable and kissed the child on the mouth. That is why we all have the indented marking above our upper lip. And if the Creator found that baby particularly beautiful, that child would be kissed on other parts of the body, and dimples would form. God would hold that baby close and whisper into her ear all the truths she would need to know to make her way back to the eternal home. Then Michael the Archangel would return the baby to the womb. By the time she was born, a veil of forgetfulness was drawn over her, and she could not recall specifically the conversation with God, but, forever, a spirit deep within her would always respond to the truths she once heard.

This myth affirmed my life experience of hearing a particular inner voice that guided me with simple clarity and renewed my conviction that, at my center, I was created around a spark of God and have the Divine dwelling within. The myth also underscored my need to discern between messages coming from my center and those seductive, destructive voices that lied to me and led me deeper into self-hatred and distrust.

For me, the way back to connectedness with God, myself, and others has been an inner journey. I have been blessed to have several companions walk with me and guide me on the way: a therapist, a spiritual director, an imaging director, and a massage therapist. I also chose to return to The College of St. Catherine to take theology classes as part of my desire to re-image God. Attending Twelve-step support groups and working with the Theological Insights Program have broadened my views and offered me the opportunity to hear other women's stories.

After a few years in therapy, I knew I needed a closer relationship with God, and I went to a place I had experienced as loving, the Cenacle Retreat Center. Besides helping me gain a better image of God, my spiritual director helped me reclaim a neglected part of myself when she encouraged me to visit my inner landscape. For a long time I had been emphasizing the rational, logical side of me, even though I naturally inclined toward the intuitive and value-centered approach to life. With the support of my therapist and spiritual director, I felt safe enough to risk revisiting the past to gain knowledge of the wounds that needed healing. I was fortunate to learn imaging from another mentor. Imaging is based on the belief that we are created around a spark of God in a deeply centered place called the Stillpoint, where Beauty, Truth, Goodness, Joy, and Peace reside. The Stillpoint has three ways of communicating with us: through spontaneous images, through dreams, and through physical symptoms. Imaging has been very helpful for me, and I would like to share a few more of my images.

One of the earliest dreams that I can recall on my inner journey had a particularly strong energy for me. Dreaming that I was asleep in my home and that I heard a gnawing sound, I went downstairs and discovered that the noise came from the basement. A faint light shone in the playroom. When I descended, I saw that an armadillo had gnawed a hole in the foundation wall and was dragging children's toys through the hole into a space beyond, from which came the source of the light. I felt drawn to the golden peach glow but was afraid to look into the hole. I watched for a while and then said, "Well, it seems I have an armadillo in my basement. Hmmm. Now I'm going back to sleep."

I recalled the dream easily because of the energy it held, but it took me years to live into its meaning. I now believe it was an invitation to bring childhood memories out of the darkness into the light where they can be healed. My dreams and images are messages to me from my Stillpoint, and sometimes my conscious mind is not ready for that enlightenment. I trust that, if I do not understand, the message will be delivered in various forms until I do understand.

My spiritual director advised me to bring Jesus into scenes from my past that were too scary to walk into alone. This has formed a rich source of prayer for me. When I use my imagination in prayer, I am somehow gifted with images that my deliberate, conscious mind would not create. I recall a time when I wanted to tell two family members of my anger toward them. I decided to do this by imagination, taking

Jesus with me. We were all sitting in darkness. I had hardly begun to express my anger when the two family members rose silently, walked out, and shut the door. I felt so abandoned and alone. Then I sensed that someone was still there in the darkness with me, and I realized it was Jesus. I asked, "Are you still here?" "Yes, I am," came the reply. "You didn't leave me?" "No, I did not leave you." And a favorite line of scripture came to my mind: "I have loved you with an everlasting love, and I am constant in my affection for you" (Jeremiah 31:3). Remembering that led me to ask Jesus, "You really love me, don't you?" He answered simply, "Yes, I really love you." And then He sat in the darkness with me for a long time.

I once dreamed that I went to a luncheon with my mother and sisters. Mother sat alone at the head of the table. Having a funny story I wanted to share, I sat on her left. One by one, my sisters came to the table but did not listen to my story. One of them wanted to sit where I was and nudged me closer to mother. When the story was finished, I looked for a place to sit, but no place was set for me. I told them that, and no one responded. I awoke weeping. When I shared that dream with my spiritual director, she suggested I take Jesus into that scene with me. I showed Him what happened, and He silently walked out of the French doors into the yard. I felt abandoned, then angry. Soon He was at the door, just looking at me. I wanted to tell Him off, but He walked away again. I stood there, feeling puzzled and resentful, and then He came to the door once more and gave a sideways nod of His head. It finally hit me; He wasn't leaving me. He wanted me to follow! He walked across the large lawn up a hill where He joined hands with people in a circular Greek dance. I ran to be with them because they were having such fun! I stopped, ran back to tell my family to come quickly. They did not move. I felt torn between joining the dance and waiting for my family, but finally I chose to join the dance. Then I noticed that most of the dancers had no faces, but somehow that was not frightening. I came to believe they would have faces some day as I trusted others who would be family to me. As I lived into the meaning of that "dance of life" image, the dancers developed the faces of my husband, therapist, spiritual director, and close friends. In trust, I could leave old relationships that were no longer life-giving. The word "community" began to develop new meanings as I experienced solidarity.

Although that image was hopeful for me, progressing from separation to connectedness, from disintegration to wholeness, from chaos to serenity can be a transition of terrible loneliness. In darkness, choosing life confirms the possibility that light still exists, even though it cannot yet be seen. Choosing to believe, even in the midst of desolation, that hope and love exist in me became a bridge of faith spanning the canyon of despair. The whole process seemed graced as I was upheld and tenderly carried by a power I call Creator, Redeemer, Comforter, and Friend.

Paradox and mystery crowd my journey. Something in me resists the inconsistencies and rests in the mystery of grace. By gradually learning to embrace images and dreams—even nightmares—as messengers from my Stillpoint, I have found new ways to connect with my deepest self. As that bond deepens, I am learning to cooperate with the Creator in giving birth to and reparenting myself. I discover daily that the spiritual life is not a rush to a predetermined destination, but an ongoing, graced process of dying and rising to life.

This brings me back to the Cross. I still do not like to meditate upon Jesus' suffering on the cross. However, I am coming closer to understanding and feeling the Love. Once I was gifted with this image: Jesus was hanging on the cross again, and I could not stand to see the pain. I took Him down, removed the crown of thorns, and cleaned His wounds. After tucking Him into a clean bed in a quiet room, I sat in the rocking chair and watched over Him as He slept. When He awoke, He did something that amazed me. He removed a crown of thorns from my head and cleaned wounds I did not know I had. He then tucked me into a clean bed in a quiet room, where I could hear birds singing as I fell asleep in luxurious safety.

Paradox has been characteristic of my recovery from deep wounds. I experience both fullness and emptiness, both surrender and resistance, both desolation and refreshing consolation. Most days I am deeply grateful that I chose to let faith help me bridge the abyss. Some days I feel as if I still crawl on that wood, crossing other chasms on my journey.

I attempted for many years to "do" life perfectly and independently. I have found, as I connect with my deepest self, that I grow more intimate with God and others. I believe we are created for community, to walk with one another through joys and sorrows, sharing our gifts. Our lives are a sacred scripture, and, when we tell our story or receive another's, we stand on Holy Ground.

Christin Lore Weber, in her book, *Blessings*, says, "Who we shall become we are already in our souls." Her book on the Beatitudes ends with this poem:

We who stand at the threshold
Peering into the dark,
Offering the shell, the rock, the flower, the song,
We who suffer the persecutions of the centuries,
       to remember, to transform, to learn compassion,
       to give birth,
We bear Justice like a silver bird in our wombs;
And she will be born.
And she will fly before us as blessing into the unknown.
And we will follow
Seeing.[1]

1. Christin Lore Weber, *Blessings* (San Francisco: Harper & Row, 1989), 199.

Authority Is a Process

Sharon Horgan

To say that I am an American Roman Catholic woman is to frame the religious and cultural context from which I examine the concept of authority. I don't get high on incense as another woman claimed to do; in fact, incense makes me sneeze. But I know that Roman Catholicism is one of the dominant genes I inherited from my parents and, in turn, passed on to my four sons. Whether that trait will remain dominant or become recessive remains to be seen. The blood that courses through my veins is O negative R.C.

The parochialism in which I grew up was a stable environment offering the comfort of knowing that I belonged and security in a game plan for life that promised fulfillment and happiness. By the time I graduated from college in 1967, I knew the game, the players, and all the rules. I had experienced the authority of church, country, and family as trustworthy and good and so consistent that they were practically indistinguishable. We had elected a Catholic president and were saying the Mass in English. Together, these sources epitomized for me the best of human achievement and human possibilities. I entered adulthood with the assurance that selfless commitment to church, country and family would be my ticket to salvation. I was confident and felt well prepared to face and embrace all that life would offer.

Within thirteen months after graduation from college, I had accomplished all the goals which I had set for myself in this life. I had a career with a job in my field of medical technology. I had married a good Catholic man and had given birth to our first son.

For a very brief period of time marked by a rather euphoric serenity, I could say with the poet, "God's in the heaven, all's right with the world." Today I can look back on that period of my life and smile as I see the narrowness of my perceptions and recognize a developmental stage characterized by self-centeredness and an uncritical, nonreflective acceptance of cultural mores and values. But I also know that what I believed to be true at that time was largely consistent with my experience. Until my life experience contradicted my assumptions, I would not change and I would not grow. There are two ways of going through life. One is the search for certitude marked by a concern for security; the other is a voyage of discovery. I had certainty, and until that certitude was lost, I could not begin the voyage of discovery. Three faith crises set me on that journey.

When our first-born child was three weeks old, I experienced the first faith crisis of my life. He was diagnosed with spinal meningitis. Because of the severity of the infection, his stage of development, and his weight (six pounds), the prognosis was grim. However, Jeff survived the illness with no side effects and today is a healthy twenty-year-old college student.

But during his illnesses, my image of reality was shattered. Life was not fair. This was my reward for being good all my life! Where was the all-good, all-powerful, all-loving God, on whom I had been told that I could always depend? My powerlessness in this situation filled me with fear and a frantic rage, the intensity of which I had never known. I alternately blamed God and myself for the situation because one of us should have been in control. This should not have happened to me, to Jeff. What had I done to deserve this? I cried for my child and for myself as I cared for him. Soothing and caressing him helped to soothe and caress me. I held him close, and, during the experience of being with my child in his struggle for life, I began to shape an understanding of the way God loves us.

When the crisis had passed, I could look back at that critical period with its confusion and emotional intensity and attempt to sort it out. I had to let go of an image of God that claimed "Him" to be all-powerful. An "Omni" God, omnipotence, omniscience, no longer made sense or held meaning for me. This Omni God of my youth gave way to a God characterized by love and understanding. I gained some insights into myself as well. My own spirituality seemed to be shallow. A lifetime of following the rules, doing good things for other people, and storing up indulgences (just in case) were selfishly motivated to prove to God and myself that I was lovable and to keep divine wrath at bay. No longer did I have the security of certitude. I embarked on the voyage of discovery because my life experience compelled me.

As I was groping for some answers to the issues of spirituality that had been raised, a different crisis arose. Pope Paul VI issued his encyclical on birth control, *Humanae Vitae.* I, as well as many Catholic married couples, received the document with dismay. The document generated for us a crisis with the moral teaching authority of the Catholic church. For myself, this crisis was the flip side of my first one. While the first crisis had dealt with my understanding and expectations of God, this crisis had to do with God's understanding and expectations of me. This only makes sense if one realizes the high esteem in which we as Catholics held the pope and the teaching authority of the church. I had not made clear distinctions between God and the pope, between Divine will and papal teaching authority.

When I was studying in my Catholic college, birth control was the hot topic in moral debates. Since a commission had been set up to discuss the issue in Rome, it could be discussed in Catholic colleges. I knew all the principal arguments, and I, along with many others, was certain that the encyclical would permit at least some legitimate uses of artificial contraception. But *Humanae Vitae* only repeated an earlier prohibition against all artificial means of regulating birth in marriage.

I knew my life situation better than the pope. I knew the moral arguments in favor of relaxing the prohibition. I could not give intellectual assent to this teaching or follow it in my own marriage. Now I was breaking the rules of the game. If the image of a powerful and controlling God could be rejected as untenable in light of my experience, then a church teaching reflecting this image of control and power could not claim authority for me either. I remembered what the Apostle Paul said to the Corinthians at the close of his treatise on love, "When I was a child, I used to talk like a child, think like a child, reason like a child. When I became an adult, I put childish ways aside" (1 Cor. 13:12). In asserting legitimate self-interest, on which I reflected in light of the moral thought of the Catholic theologians of the day, I made my first leap as a responsible moral agent into religious adulthood. Taking ownership of my own sexuality, along with responsibility for my marriage and my family, was a liberating experience. Love replaced law as the standard by which to make moral decisions. It was only after I took this step toward independence that I could recognize my own dependence on external sources of authority in my own life.

The third authority crisis was occasioned by the 1976 declaration by the Sacred Congregation for the Doctrine of the Faith on the Question of the Admission of Women to the Ministerial Priesthood. I had thought that I had no great stake in this issue. I had no realistic expectations that the centuries-old tradition of celibate male priesthood was about to change. The declaration was issued in response to a number of voices being raised in this country critiquing the tradition as an injustice to women in the Roman Catholic church. It was not the conclusion of the declaration that was so wounding to me, and it was not that I myself had experienced a call to the ordained priesthood. I was married and expecting my fourth son. It was the reasons given in the document that were extremely alienating to me as a woman: that there would not be a "natural resemblance," which must exist between Christ and his minister if the role of Christ were not taken by a man"; that when "Christ himself, the author of the Covenant, the Bridegroom and head of the church, is represented exercising his ministry of salvation . . . his role must be taken by a man"; and that the difference "does not stem from a personal superiority of the latter in the order of values, but only from a difference in fact on the level of functions and service."[1]

I am still stung when I read those words. The document, however, was very revealing for me because it illustrated how deeply our attitudes impact on our understanding of reality. Sexism exists in the authority structures of the church. I can neither minimize this sexism nor ignore it. My insights about authority are shaped, in part, by how my experiences conflict with the sexist authority of the church.

The experiences that I have described are uniquely mine, and yet I think they are representative of contemporary women's experiences with the various Jewish and Christian authority structures. Many of us have experienced the void of meaningful feminine God images within our worship and devotional resources. Sexism has colored Christianity's interpretation of the deposit of faith in moral and dogmatic teaching. And exclusion from ministry and discrimination in ministerial appointments are common to many women within our religious heritages. But perhaps there is a misconception in my assumption that authority is a static and concrete entity. I realize that authority reflects an ongoing dialogue, a process, a dynamism that functions within the living community of believers as we journey through history. Because there is a need for legitimate authority in the church, there is a magisterium, an official teaching office, which functions only in dynamic relation with the received sources of revelation and the living community of believers. Therefore, there are limits to the authority exercised by the magisterium. John Macquarrie in *Principles of Christian Theology* describes four qualifiers to ecclesiastical authority that I will apply to my consideration of women's experience.[2]

In the first place, ecclesiastical authority is a derived authority, stemming from Jesus Christ and ultimately responsible to him. The community that shaped the tradition and created the Scriptures is, in turn, subject to scriptural authority. It is helpful to return to the roots of our tradition, to the Exodus experience as described in the Pentateuch. The liberation from slavery was followed by the wilderness period. During this time, when the Hebrew people were formed into the people of God, conflict existed between the authority of God and the authority of their leader, Moses. These experiences helped to shape them into the chosen People of God. When the Second Vatican Council employed the metaphor of the "People of God" in describing the church, they were acknowledging that the church too is journeying towards the fullness of truth and life but is not yet the People of God in the fullest sense of the word.

When feminist theologians and biblical scholars bring their recognition of the sin of sexism to their work, they are contributing to the ongoing journey of the pilgrim church as the People of God. In applying their skills to the texts we have received, they are recovering feminine imagery that has been ignored in translation and interpretation. They point out the stories within the Bible that critique the dominant patriarchy. Their efforts represent a constructive critique of biblical misogyny that has contributed to the oppression of women in church and society.

The second limit on the magisterium of the church is the fact that the authority of the teaching office requires consensus. The community should authorize the leadership of the church by assenting to the truth of its teachings. This action of the Spirit in the church, as it grapples over issues regarding its self-understanding and its role in the world, is grounded in the lived human experience of the whole community.

If the experience of a significant minority of the community is one of suffering, oppression, alienation, or persecution, it falls within what theologians call a "contrast experience." Although this experience is largely negative, it contains an insight that calls for the kind of practice that can create a new future. The process can be described as an initial experience of dissonance, of the absence of what "ought to be," which then yields a dim but definite sense of what one should do here and now. The prophetic insight and voice of the church has its origin in the contrasts that exist within the living experience of those who are touched by actual injustice and who are struggling against it. Women sensitized to their experience of injustice in the church continue to offer prophetic insight to the whole church by calling for teaching, order and practice, which will reflect more truly and faithfully the church's claim to be sacrament to the world.

Macquarrie's third qualifier is that the authority of the church is made relevant by the historical and cultural factors within which it functions. At the core of our heritage is the belief that God chose history as a medium of revelation. Salvation history continues as we participate in the journey of the People of God.

For those of us conscious of the sin of sexism, we must witness creatively and critique constructively, or we are guilty of obstructing the history of salvation. Our culture has been dominated by what Anne Wilson Schaef describes as the "White Male System."[3] Her work clarifies for me how my church and I have been affected by this cultural reality. Sexism is perpetuated by women and men who are caught in a system that views reality solely from the position and perspective of white men. I recognize in my own experiences that elitism is an attitudinal tendency to which I am tempted. This attitude derives from the myth that the White Male System (WMS) is innately superior to any other system that might exist. My temptation to be dependent on external sources for the affirmation of myself and what I choose to do is derived from being acculturized as a woman in this system. When I deny the truth of my experience as woman, I capitulate to the WMS. When I live according to the stereotypical definitions of the system, I submit to it and authorize it.

When we, as women, bring our experiences, feelings and intuitions into our own discernment processes, we open up a whole universe of knowledge and meaning not available to those locked into the WMS where objectivity, logic, and reason are the only sources for truth. All experiences of oppression and alienation are more clearly understood and exposed as evil when we are attentive to the emerging Female System that we are beginning to recognize and claim as our own. The WMS encourages us to play out our role of victims, powerlessly stuck in self-pity for our woundedness. The emerging Female System calls us to be martyr-witnesses to the truth of our being and our experience of reality. Careful discernment and disciplined, courageous action will prevent us from being submerged in the dominant culture and will contribute to the unshackling of the church from bondage to the WMS.

Macquarrie's fourth criterion, limiting the teaching authority of the church, is that every authoritative utterance needs to be tested for intellectual integrity.

As women become empowered through experience and education and feminist scholars and theologians gain credibility with ecclesiastical leadership, women's influence will enrich and enhance the whole church. In recognizing and accepting my own intellectual integrity, I cannot in honesty accept any source of authority that cannot meet these criteria, nor can I expect this of others.

The Dogmatic Constitution on the Church (*Lumen Gentium*) stresses the right and the duty of lay people to speak out freely on matters concerning not only the secular world but also the church if they enjoy a particular competence. This emphasis is repeated in the *Decree on the Laity* and the *Pastoral Constitution on the Church in the Modern World*. The *Pastoral Constitution on the Church in the Modern World* (*Gaudium et Spes*) also calls all of us to build a new humanity.[4] As women we need to claim this responsibility more assertively. We will receive a hearing to the extent that we reveal in our lives our dedication to the Gospel of Jesus Christ and to the mission of the church.

It is now apparent to me, in reflective dialogue with the larger Catholic tradition, that the authoritative process in which we participate calls us to challenge the authority structures of our church and calls us to an integrated fidelity, to ourselves, to God, to the church, and to the human family. A short transitional verse in the Gospel of Luke that serves as a paradigm for me is the one which separates the infancy narrative from the baptism and ministry of Jesus: "And Jesus grew in wisdom, age and grace before God and the human family" (Luke 2:52). The process through which Jesus came to be recognized as the ultimate authority included conflicts with the authority of his family, his religious community, and religious and political figures of his day. He even had conflicts with his friends and followers who did not understand the meaning of his teaching and life. Luke shows the role that women played in their relationships with him. A woman washed his feet with her tears. Women stood at the foot of the cross in solidarity with his suffering and vulnerability. Women, in their grief, went to the tomb to anoint the dead body of Jesus and witnessed the truth of the Resurrection. And women as well as men gathered in the upper room to receive the spirit of Christ that formed the first community of disciples.

The authoritative process that empowered the original women disciples of Jesus continues to empower us.

---

1. As quoted in *Women and Priesthood*, Carroll Stuhlmueller, ed. (Collegeville: Liturgical Press, 1978), 212-225.

2. John Macquarrie, *Principles of Christian Theology* (New York: Charles Scribner's Sons, 1977).

3. Anne Wilson Schaef, *Women's Reality* (Minneapolis: Winston Press, 1981).

4. Walter M. Abbott, ed., *The Documents of Vatican II* (New York: Guild Press, 1966).

7.

Anger:
Chaotic and Creative

*I have tried to avoid my anger. In spite of myself,
I am in that stage now, but I am no longer afraid of anger.
I find it to be a creative, transforming force; anger is
a stage I must go through if I am ever to get to
what lies beyond.*

MARY KAYE MEDINGER
Theological Insights, October 9, 1987

Being Faithful
to My Anger

Mary Lou Judd Carpenter

My life has been lived on two levels, as if I lived in two different worlds. In my external, visible existence as an adult, I am considered a good woman, conscientious, helpful, organized. My hidden, internal life finds voice in the terrified little girl within me. She is scared of not measuring up to the expectations and needs of others and is fearful of sharing her tender and vulnerable narrative. As an adult, although anxious about revealing myself, I will give a short narrative of my life. Then I will invite the child within me to tell *her* story, before I reflect further on what listening to the child has taught the adult.

For my first forty years, I was seldom angry, hurt or sad, joyful or peaceful. I was born in 1934 in Rochester, Minnesota. My parents delighted in a firstborn child. When I was eight months old, my father completed his surgery training, and we moved to China where he was returning a second time as a medical missionary. We crossed the Pacific by boat and proceeded to Peking (now known as Beijing). Mother and I stayed there for eight months, so she could attend Chinese language school.

Dad continued into the interior of North China to run a large city hospital in Fenchow. This was my first significant separation from him. I was also somewhat separated from Mom, as I was cared for by an *Amah*, a Chinese nursemaid, while Mom was busy studying the language and culture. I was almost eighteen months old when finally we

118

were living together in our family home in Fenchow.

During the next two years, my family was separated several times because of disruptions and dislocations from attacks by bands of Chinese Communists. Eventually the Japanese militarists attacked and captured Fenchow, forcing women and children to return to the United States. But the Japanese allowed my father to remain in Fenchow to run the hospital and provide medical care while we went to stay with my maternal grandparents in New Jersey.

With my mother and my two-year-old sister, Carolyn, I was separated from the language and customs I had known and, for a year, from Dad. My youngest sister, Ellie, was born several months later, and I was the good, helpful oldest sister, age four.

When Dad finally came back from China, he was still away from our family most of the time, speaking all over the country about his fears of possible aggression by Japanese militarists against the United States. Eventually discouraged by public apathy, he returned to practicing medicine, and we moved to Minneapolis.

One year later, the Japanese attack on Pearl Harbor swept America into World War II. Concerned citizens wanted the federal government to benefit from his experiences in Asia and elected him to represent them in Congress. We moved again—to Washington.

I continued to be obedient, careful, helpful. I was keenly aware of the importance of being good; "difficulties" were not acceptable in the families of elected officials in the 1940s. I wanted to do my part, so Dad could help the country. Growing in independence and competence in high school, I was already becoming a grand overachiever.

My education continued at Mount Holyoke College in Massachusetts. Living up to the standards set by my parents, I graduated with academic honors and as president of my class. I took a job in New York City, but my own internal agenda was to follow the prescribed societal path for women: to marry, raise good children like myself, and thus secure a satisfying life. Within a year I accomplished my dream of marrying a nice young man and went to secretarial school to be able to support him in law school. After he graduated in 1960, we moved to Minneapolis with our one-year-old son. We bought a house, had a daughter, had a second daughter, and settled into the supposedly ideal life. I got involved in many community projects and at church.

But dissatisfactions and resentments were growing in me. I experienced unhappiness in my marriage and frustration in the part of me that found identity and ego-satisfaction in achievements and success. Volunteer work was challenging, but I was envious of people with careers and power. I spent my energy trying to mold my family.

Shortly after my fortieth birthday, a friend suggested I join a group of women who were exploring their feelings. I went along. The leader asked me about the role of alcohol in my family. I was concerned about my husband's drinking, but I did not think it affected me too seriously. The leader asked what I was doing about it. I said, "Nothing." He quietly commented that he was glad he was not in a family with a "bitch" like me, because I would let such an ill person die. I was stunned and scared, but I listened, asked for help, and worked with assessment professionals. In a few weeks, our family was involved in a rehabilitation program for victims of alcoholism.

In the treatment process, I was confronted about my limited emotional development and the absence of a "feeling life" in me. When I was given an assignment to list my personal needs, I could not come up with *any* inner needs. But those powerful, internal, angry feelings seemed to be getting more insistent. The massive wall that had been built to separate me from my inner way of knowing (my feelings) was crumbling.

As I got involved in Alanon, therapy, "growth" groups, prayer groups, and individual spiritual direction, I began to realize how much pain I felt. I learned about being powerless rather than powerful, about the difference between helplessness and hopelessness, about surrender rather than success.

My fury increased: about having been alienated from such an important part of myself; about the blindness in my original family and the limitations in my present family; about the injustices experienced in so many patriarchal systems and perpetuated by the compliance of women like me with cultural rules and roles. I ranted at God, raved with trusted friends and confidants. I became increasingly aware and scared of my feelings, while struggling to find appropriate ways to express and deal with them.

Some consolation came when I found in the Old Testament almost four hundred instances when God is angry. If I believe the Genesis account that *we are made in God's image and likeness,* surely I was to accept my human angers. But I wrestled with the reality that I had chosen a traditional path of female dependency. In the same way that over-dependency can become detrimental to a relationship, so my growth into better mental health harmed a relationship that was not healthy in the beginning, my marriage. The day after my fiftieth birthday, my husband moved out. Two years later we were divorced.

I was very hurt and hostile about the ending of my marriage, even though I tried to remember that there is no such thing as a *failure* except a *mistake* from which nothing is learned. I was mad about the suffering of my children and friends. I was fearful about economic inequities and necessary changes in my lifestyle. I was scared about becoming invisible, being left out of the family/couple orientation of our culture and of the church. I was angry that I had been unable to express my thoughts and feelings in ways that could be understood and that might have changed outcomes.

I took a job in a church as a lay assistant for pastoral care, while my own personal work continued with a therapist and a spiritual director, two safe people with whom I could risk being authentic about my feelings. I learned that, behind anger, an unconscious hurt or fear exists, usually triggered by someone else's behavior. I discovered that anger can be a sign of mental health, if a person's identity or integrity has been submerged or lost in a relationship. After two years, I left my job for travel to Sri Lanka, India, and Nepal. Gradually, I became more reflective. Some of my anger about hurts and losses from my divorce began to dissipate. Healing began.

My children were settling into adulthood when I helped my elderly parents move out of their Washington home. While packing, they found old letters filled with vivid accounts of our experiences during the many separations during those first six years of my life. Since I had almost no memories of those times, I asked them questions about my childhood. They talked matter-of-factly about events that seemed significant to them but which had been traumatic for a youngster. My curiosity increased about those early years in China, and a gnawing sadness swelled inside of me.

My parents had coped with those chaotic events in adult ways, and I found out that my childlike emotional responses had not been welcomed or approved amid the disruptions and flight. My feelings were "trained" out of me. As I realized that I was emotionally separated from that little girl, I yearned to know what it had been like for her. I longed to reconnect with that missing part of me.

To help me get acquainted with her, I sought a concrete representation of that child. I met with a woman who made caricature dolls from pictures of children. I showed her my newly discovered pictures and shared with her what life had been like for that three-year-old. She listened compassionately. Over several weeks, she gently brought into being a likeness of that youngster, even finding clothes almost identical to what I wore in one of the pictures.

What a weird and wonderful sensation for me to hold that young child, to know and befriend her. The doll accompanied me to a retreat on "The Wounded Child in the Adult." Together we read more letters about those early experiences, weeping, giggling, and growing to love one another. As I learned how she had coped and survived, I was awed. I have reassured her that the grown-up Mary Lou will not abandon her this time, and that she will be safe, as now she tells her story.

My Mommy and Daddy are very happy when I am born. Even though I am colicky and fussy, they love me. But we leave Rochester and go to a new place, and I am confused by the different talk and the strange sounds and smells. Daddy disappears for a long time, and I don't see Mommy much because a Chinese lady takes care of me.

Soon Mommy gets sick and has my little sister. The very next night, after Carolyn is born, we run away from the soldiers who are coming to fight in our city. I ride in a very cold car with my new Amah. When we get to the next town, I am left with the Amah, as Daddy goes back to the hospital in the old city, and Mommy and Carolyn go to the hospital in the new town. I feel deserted. Soon the soldiers are coming here too, so we flee to Peking, riding thirty-three hours on a train jammed with refugees. I am sick—and scared.

After six months, we go back to our house in Fenchow. I am lonely, as there are no playmates, and Carolyn is too little to be any fun. Mommy is busy teaching piano, and Daddy works hard helping the sick people. I help by putting away the laundry, and I know where everything belongs. My parents are very proud of me.

By summertime, everyone is talking again about more fighting and bombings. Now the worst has happened: we have to leave all my toys and my house. It is scary to hide in bomb shelters, but I try to be brave. When we are escaping on the train, it is very dark because we are hiding from the planes. There are lots of wounded soldiers on the train and not much food. I have nothing to play with.

Finally, after a day and a half, we get off in Hankow. Now we have to find an airplane to take us to Hong Kong. We wait a long time, seven days, before we leave. Why isn't Daddy coming with us? Why does he have to go back to the hospital? Isn't there anyone else who can help the hurt people?

In Hong Kong, I throw up a lot, from all the excitement, Mommy says. I don't want to go to America—I want to go back to China, to my house and Daddy. But I am being "good."

I hate the boat. Mommy is very sick. She is growing another baby inside, and the boat rolls over all the time. I hate having to take care of Carolyn. I am mad. Mommy spanks me a lot and doesn't understand when I am naughty and noisy. I don't like being bad, but I can't help it. Mommy is very unhappy and worried, too.

When we get to New Jersey on Thanksgiving Day, Mommy is very glad. But I am sad. People talk and look different. Daddy writes me a special letter. In part, it says this:

"I want to wish you a Happy Birthday. You will be four years and will understand most everything now. I am sure Mother has told you about the little, teeny, weeny baby who is coming to live with you. Daddy would like to be there, but he can't—and he hopes especially much that Mary Lou will work hard to help Grandma while Mother is going to the hospital, and when Mother comes home, will work even harder to do all sorts of errands for her, and let Mother have time to rest and sleep and take care of the little baby. I know you will try hard every day. You have brought Daddy so much joy and happiness and gladness these four years since you were born. And I know each year as you grow bigger, Daddy will be all the more glad and proud and happy because of his own Mary Lou. Goodbye, my sweet daughter."

What a nice Daddy I have. I try hard to be good and helpful. I know children are to be seen and not heard, but I wish there was someone to help me. Everyone is too busy, and I mustn't disturb them. Actually, the new baby is rather a bother.

Now it has been a year since I saw my Daddy. When he comes off the train, Mommy says to run and hug him. But he speaks in strange ways. I don't know him, and I am shy. He is very worried about the war and soon goes away all the time to talk to people.

When we move to Minneapolis, I try not to be too afraid. Mommy is sick again because she is growing twins. They are born too soon, and they die. This is the first time I see Daddy cry. Mommy has to stay in the hospital. I help Daddy by picking out the tiny dresses for Marjorie and Barbara to wear in the casket.

Daddy is busy taking care of his patients, and then he talks and argues with people about the wars within China and with Japan. He really wants all people to be free, and that is a good idea. So we are moving to Washington, D.C., where he can help the country.

It is scary to go into the new fourth grade classroom in the middle of the year, when everyone already has friends. My family just saw the movie "Little Women." It made me cry and cry, because that family is not at all like mine. I feel very separate from my parents and sisters. My parents are doing important things. My sisters just gang up on me. When we go back to Minneapolis in the summers, some people say Daddy is wrong about the world, and it is bad to have him as their congressman, and he should be defeated. Is that right? So many questions make my head swim. I am tired of trying to figure things out. I think it is better if I just keep quiet and be invisible. It seems as if no one notices anyway.

> Now in high school, Mary Lou is a cheerleader and rather smart and I am left behind. She seems very grown-up when she leaves for college. She really hasn't paid much attention to me for years. She is strong and competent and organized and good. I am sad and mad and bratty, and I get in her way. She doesn't want me, or to know what I know, or feel what I feel. I think I'll take a twenty-year snooze, like Rip Van Winkle. Perhaps she will want me later.

Thus, the separation between my child self and my adult self became complete. As an adult, I marched on valiantly—the ultimate caretaker, doing good works, and faithfully attending to the needs of my husband and kids. There was no room in life for spontaneity nor permission for playfulness. I was efficient and dedicated, committed to serving and being useful. My controlling manner and judgmental opinions did cause problems for the family, but my three children did well negotiating the perils of growing up.

Little Mary Lou was surprised several years ago when she began to hear rumbles from me, queries about her whereabouts. She was leery about requests to come forth with her perceptions. My parents' gifts of letters and reminiscences facilitated the process of a gradual reconnecting. Little Mary Lou began to trust adult Mary Lou, as we remembered the events of those early years. We discovered a respectful rhythm that balanced each of our preferences and needs. Slowly came a miraculous healing of the divided parts of Mary Lou. The reintegration of the two sources of wisdom—facts and feelings—allows the united voices to speak together as one now.

What have I learned? I understand that feelings are facts, neither good nor bad but simply information. In my early life my feelings were not validated or affirmed. I did get approval when I was good and acted grown-up. So I disowned difficult feelings and did what I was told in order to stay connected with my parents. My own need to be a kid who could goof off and let others care for me was buried under a lifetime of worrying about other family members. I was a little adult at a young age, but underneath, I was mad, with no clues or modeling on how to deal with this chaos.

Since I was separated from the feeling part of myself that could be authentic and honest, I did not know that I was hurt, scared or angry. I thought I was just fine, thank you. I directed my primary efforts toward protecting others and preserving harmony in relationships with family and friends.

Anger is something all of us feel. Anger exists for a reason and deserves our respect and attention. It is a sign that something is wrong and signals the need for change. Many of our problems with anger occur when we choose between having a relationship and having a self. We learn to hide our anger because it often brings the disapproval of others. We learn to betray and sacrifice the self in order to preserve harmony with others. Women are especially susceptible to ignoring and burying anger. As we deny our awareness and expression of anger, we do not see clearly, think precisely, or remember freely. Many of us focus our attention on trying to change someone else. We lose ourselves.

When I functioned in the outside world without access to that large source of information, my feelings, I surely lived out of the hidden rage of my buried self. In my forties, as I began to connect with my internal reality and started to acknowledge my anger, I did not know how to express it appropriately. I did not know that my anger did not mean someone else was to blame. It took years before I understood, with Harriet Lerner, that "anger is a tool for change when it challenges us to become more of an expert on the self and less of an expert on others."[1]

Jesus said, "Know the truth and the truth will set you free" (John 8:32). In earlier years, I had interpreted this to mean seeking the truth about other people or situations. I was unable to pursue the truth in *me* because that path led me into guilt and shame. Guilt and shame were intolerable for someone who was as "good" and "useful" as I believed I was. I even viewed my perfectionism as a virtue. When attending a retreat on "Effective Living," I was astonished to hear perfectionism described as a character defect and a sign of low self-esteem!

Religious understandings can interfere with our self-acceptance if we have been taught that God judges feelings harshly. I found courage and consolation in biblical prophets like Jeremiah, who cried out to God: "I did not sit celebrating in the circle of merrymakers. Under the weight of your hand I sat alone, because you filled me with indignation" (Jeremiah 15:17).

I cannot overestimate the importance of spiritual direction for me these past fifteen years. Five differently gifted, loving women have journeyed with me in my search for myself and for God. And two caring, creative therapists taught me psychological wisdom and helped me focus on my own life when I wanted to find answers and solutions outside myself.

My tenaciousness has kept me on the pilgrimage. When people were puzzled because I wasn't "recovering" after my divorce by moving ahead into a new life. I tried hard not to feel judged or inadequate. My priority was to continue attending with honesty and integrity to the angers and bitterness inside. To me, life is about being faithful to an on-going process, not heading toward some ideal destination.

In the midst of this work and struggle, my "wounded child" timidly ventured out from an unknown part of me. She brought insights and remembrances of my long-ago experiences, offering feelings that had been languishing in the shadows of darkness. As this information came forth into the light, it was as a new morning beginning, a dawning.

As it dawns on (and in) me, with the simplicity and openness of the little child, I make new meanings of my life. I understand why I gave up playfulness and creativity, how I became excessively compulsive in my competence and achieving, and how my angers became huge and dominating. I examine old family patterns and learn more about the ways in which I carried the angers of other women, as if part of my genetic inheritance.

As my recovery and healing continue, I have setbacks. It is challenging to keep the habit-ridden adult Mary Lou from riding roughshod over little Mary Lou. Or, it is tempting to give in to the little girl's fears and frustrations, which I experience more freely now. So I work to remain connected with both parts of myself, to maintain an equilibrium between the two energies. I like the Chinese symbol of the Yin and the Yang, both segments interacting to influence life.

Thus, out of the chaos of my interior feelings comes the possibility of new creation. What people do not tell us is that in our fifties, we have a repeat of our adolescence. Our bodies change without our permission, our family structures change as parents die and children leave home, and our rules and roles change.

Women are taking more responsibility and enjoying greater freedom. Since we have not yet been trained for this, it is natural to have periods of awkwardness and uncertainty, as we try new behaviors and dream of fresh possibilities. With more assimilation and integration of our "little child" and our "adult self," we will bring greater wholeness to our living and to our relationships.

As we befriend our "inner child," there is new meaning in the Old Testament description of the peaceable kingdom as a place where "a little child shall guide them" (Isaiah 11:6). Or, we find a poignant expectancy in the story of Jesus instructing his disciples to "Let the children come to me. Do not hinder them. The kingdom of God belongs to such as these" (Matthew 19:14).

1. Harriet Lerner, *The Dance of Anger* (New York: Harper and Row, 1985), 102.

Coming Home through Anger

Chris Franke

We have all experienced in some way or other the need to adapt to changing situations. We may have said goodbye to a child leaving home to go to college or to marry; we may have experienced the pain of divorce or the loss of a spouse; we may have been the victim of abuse or sexual harrassment; perhaps we know first hand what it is like to not be one of the good old boys on the job. We all know what it is like to be displaced, deported, alienated in some way. How do we make home, or remake home, in such situations?

Let us look at how one group of people, the Israelites, made home when they were not allowed to be at home, when they were pushed out of their homes, when they were driven from their home and forced to live in an alien land. These people did two things which helped them to survive their displacement, their exile. They told and retold their stories, and they expressed their deepest feelings of anger at those who dispossessed them of their homes.

Imagine being attacked in your home by a powerful army. Picture your capital city, in this case, Jerusalem, in flames, the capitol building burned to the ground, the place where you worshipped God on fire, your homes destroyed, the walls of the city pulled down. Imagine watching as many of your family and friends were slaughtered by the enemy, and then being seized and abused by this enemy and being forced to march for hundreds of miles to a far off land where you would live as captives, aliens, everyone and everything you cherished destroyed, lost, taken away.

How did these people respond to such a situation? Psalm 137 is an example. This is a poignant and beautiful and terrible psalm expressing the anguish felt by Israelites who were wrenched from their homes.

> By the streams of Babylon there we sat;
>   loudly we wept as we remembered Zion.
> On the trees there we hung up our harps,
>   even though our captor, our tormentors,
>   asked us the words of our joyous songs.
> "Sing for us the songs of Zion!"
> But how could we sing the Lord's song
>   on alien soil?
>
> If I would forget you, O Jerusalem,
>   let my right hand be forgotten!
> Let my tongue stick to my palate
>   if I do not keep alive
>   the memory of Jerusalem!
> Keep in memory, O Lord, the sons of Edom
>   and what they did to Jerusalem.
> They said, "Tear her down,
>   tear her down to the foundations!"
> O daughter of Babylon, you destroyer,
>   blessed be the one who repays you
>   the evil you have done to us.
> Blessed be the one who seizes and smashes
>   your little ones against the rock. (translation mine)

Most of us are repelled by the sentiment in the last verse of this psalm and ask how people could express such terrible wishes. We wonder how such a disturbing and gruesome request has found its way into the Bible. Is this the kind of viewpoint we expect to find in the Bible? Why does our tradition allow such a horrible thought to stand, to be expressed? How can faithful believers identify with these feelings?

Can we in the twentieth century understand these powerful human emotions of the sixth century B.C.E.? In middle-class America, this kind of language, this kind of thinking—wishing evil upon others, and name-calling—is not polite; it is not good etiquette. People who express anger or hatred are considered immature, ethically inferior; we say they have lost control of themselves. We do not praise people for speaking this way, and it is difficult for us to listen to people who are given to such sentiments. However, the expression of anger and the vilification of the oppressor was an important part of making home for the exiled people of Israel, and, I suggest, it can be an important part of our making home when we are forced to live in exile, when we are treated as aliens.

How are we to understand the function, the working, of this expression of anger and hatred on the part of the Israelites? What does such an expression do for them? I think there are two ways to understand this.

First, it reflects real emotion, the feelings of hostility and anger that the people of Israel had toward their oppressors. They did not hide these passionate feelings; they did not deceive themselves or anyone else about the depth of their emotions. Such expressions need not be considered inferior or immature. In fact, I would suggest that a person forced from her or his home who did not feel hostility might be engaging in some kind of self-deception.

There is a second way to understand the function of this expression of anger and hatred, this wish for the death of the Babylonians and Edomites and their children. The expression of anger and hostility in Psalm 137 can also have a social function. It defines this group of people as different from their oppressors. It challenges the legitimacy of the oppressors and joins the Israelites in a common cause against the values of the Babylonians who have snatched them from their homes. This community stands together in supportive opposition against its enemy.

For people whose social status and place have never been challenged, the act of calling down evil upon an enemy's head may seem to be pathological, distasteful. But the person who has experienced some kind of displacement can more easily understand what it means to hate one's enemy. Today there are liberation theologians who realize the social value of just such an attitude toward an oppressor. To challenge an oppressor is considered by some to be essential to the formation of new ideas, new ideologies. If an oppressor is not challenged, needed social change may not take place. To challenge an oppressor is also essential if reconciliation and forgiveness are ever to take place. Israel, by wishing evil upon the oppressor Babylon, was challenging the power of Babylon and questioning its legitimacy.

Another aspect of this psalm needs examination. The Israelites did not only express bitter hatred toward their oppressor. While this psalm laments the loss of home (Jerusalem), it, at the same time, is a powerful expression of hope. When they were asked by their captors to "sing us some of your joyful songs," the Israelites refused. Instead, the Israelites hung up their instruments and sat and wept. They refused to sing the songs of Zion, but paradoxically their refusal to sing has itself become a song. One of the things which kept them alive on alien soil was their passionate love for their home and their refusal to let that memory die.

These people knew the value of memory, of remembering. This exquisite poem, which speaks of the refusal to sing, is a song. It speaks of the urgent necessity of remembering, of telling and retelling the stories and traditions of home.

We know that these people who sat by the river and mourned the loss of home were forced to live away from Jerusalem for at least seventy years. What did they do for seventy years? How did they survive? How did they make their homes? They told stories, and they continued to live out the tradition that had been theirs before they were displaced, before the exile.

But they did not simply retell these stories exactly as they had told them before the exile. Nor did they merely repeat the traditional practices in place before their lives had been so radically disrupted by the Babylonian destruction of their homeland. The stories needed to be reinterpreted and told anew in light of the changed circumstances.

During the time of the exile, people did not enjoy peace and security in their own land. They repeated these words not only to remind themselves of what God had done for them in the past, but also as a sign of hope for the future. Just as God had brought their ancestors out of slavery in an alien land, Egypt, God would soon do the same for the Israelites who were enslaved in the alien land of Babylon. The story was reclaimed, reinterpreted, and understood from a very different perspective.

In the Bible we have evidence that faithful people did not simply write down words and slavishly remember them. In the Bible we see that in order to keep the story of the community alive, in order to maintain the tradition, in order to make home in an alien land, people retold their stories, reinterpreted and changed them so that they would continue to be meaningful to their descendants in later times.

What can we learn from the Bible about making home, or remaking home if we have been displaced, deported, or exiled from our homes? The Bible tells us that it is legitimate, perhaps even essential, to be honest about our anger and hostility in situations of oppression. Here it is, this kind of talk, right in the Bible! This rage, this hatred of the oppressor, is not limited to Psalm 137. Many of the individual psalms of lament express similar sentiments. People ask God to break the teeth of the wicked (Psalms 3 and 58), to dash them into pieces (Psalm 2), to break the arm of the evildoer (Psalm 10), to make them be like the snail that dissolves into slime (Psalm 58), and to blind people so they cannot see (Psalm 69). In the Book of Job, the innocent Job is angry and rages at his oppressors: his "friends," who accuse him rather than comfort him, and even God, who refuses to respond to his pleas.

The Bible reminds us of the importance of telling and retelling stories, of remembering all of our stories. If we are to be at home within our families, our communities, our religious traditions, we need to realize that it is appropriate, even necessary, to tell and retell our stories, our traditions, and to reinterpret the meaning of our traditions for our own day. People (women and men) who have been abused by spouse or boss, those who have been dispossessed or disenfranchised by society, those who have been unjustly excluded from full participation in religious tradition—each has a certain perspective of her or his situation. The expression of our unique experiences and understandings can add to the wealth of tradition. To the extent that we do not tell our stories, the human condition will be impoverished. To the extent that we reflect on stories of the human struggle, the human condition will be enriched.

8.

Solitude

Dip into the well of your experience. Listen to your wisdom. Connect that with the wisdom around you and with what you know. Then, in touch with your inner voice and experience, speak.

RICHELLE PEARL-KOLLER
Theological Insights, October 7, 1988

The Gift of Solitude

Linda Hutchinson

Solitude, always an important part of my Catholic religious heritage, did not become part of my spiritual practice until recently. During the first thirty-seven years of my life, my experience of solitude was not positive; it was one of isolation, an involuntary detachment from others. However, for the past six years, solitude has been an important practice in getting to know myself, being at-one with myself, embracing myself as a sexual/spiritual being. I now choose times to be alone, to be in solitude, to reclaim that part of my religious heritage.

In my early years I was in a "culture of silence," not a positive silence, but an imprisoned silence of self-negation. Solitude was something to be avoided. There were reasons for that avoidance, reasons buried deep within me. It was too scary for me to *be* in solitude. I did not like myself enough to be alone with myself, and I did not want to be alone with my God. I did not have a caring God. I had not moved beyond the God of my childhood—the white male judge up in the sky. In particular I was in conflict about my sexuality and spirituality. At an early age I had learned that sex was sinful.

I want to share three incidents from my life to illustrate my conflict with sexuality and spirituality. Around the time of my first Confession and Holy Communion, my older brother was into showing off his penis to me. Being a curious seven-year-old, I wanted to know all I could. My sister, who was the oldest, found out and told my mother.

I do not recall my mother's exact words, but, standing near the stove in the kitchen of our farm home, what I heard was: I was a bad girl, and I had committed the worst sin in the world. From then on, I was going to be good, and goodness meant not having anything to do with sex.

During my teens, I wanted to be popular and to have a boyfriend, but I was afraid to date. I was pre-occupied with kissing. What would I do if he wanted to kiss me? At catechism I had received a pamphlet explaining when kissing was a mortal sin and when it was a venial sin. I figured it was safest to avoid kissing altogether. I recall having only three dates in high school.

In the early 1980s I worked as a continuing education specialist at Hazelden facilitating workshops. Very often participants of the workshops would ask me if I was an ex-nun. I was devastated because what I heard was "Are you asexual?" Riding home in the carpool each day, I shared these incidents with my friends. One day a carpool-mate suggested that the next time someone asked me if I was an ex-nun, to just say, "Why the fuck do you ask?" Her humor was a gift, helping me to be more light-hearted, but it did not resolve my inner turmoil.

I experienced a turning point, a sexual/spiritual awakening about seven years ago when I attended a compulsivity clinic. The clinic was an abbrievated model of treatment applied to all addictions and dysfunctions. The first day the presenters took extensive histories of each of us, focusing on our family life in terms of addictions and abuse. At the end of the day we were told to listen to ourselves for messages of what we needed to know or do. We could do this in whatever way suited us. I chose to go into a room all by myself to listen. All I could hear was "I'm not gonna do this right, and I'm not gonna do enough."

So that's what I reported to group. I was asked by my therapist if I hated myself. I had never thought about it, but decided I must because of my lack of self-care. I was told to wallow in the self-hatred and see what would come up. So I did. I asked for some help from a woman in my group. When she massaged my back—more feelings moved through me. As she gave me a massage, I repeated over and over, "I hate myself, I hate myself, I hate myself."

The next day when I reported in group, the therapists noticed that every time I got close to something painful, I would go "into my head," that is, I would go numb. One of the therapists offered to hypnotize me. I agreed. Under hypnosis, I had a sense of walking down the stairs in my childhood home and no one being there. I felt all alone, that no one was there for me. Later that day during a relaxation/meditation of returning to the womb, I imagined the comfort of the womb and the fear and sadness of entering a world where I wasn't wanted. My mother already had three small children and an alcoholic husband. She didn't need another "gift from God." I got angry at God and thought, "If they don't want me, why the heck am I here." My therapist had offered to hypnotize me again if I wanted, and I could choose to go back to whatever age I wanted. So the next day in group, I said I wanted to go back to the time when I or someone decided I was coming into this world and find out *what for*. It was the first time I took that question seriously: why am I here?

Earlier that day I had done more work with massage moving the feelings up and out. The therapists had described how often we store shame in our pelvic area, anger in our stomach, fear in our chest, and confusion in our heads. It made sense. I observed it working in others and I could feel it in myself.

My shame and anger were loose and moving, but there was something stuck in my throat. I also had strong sensations in my hands. The therapist discouraged my idea of being hypnotized back to a time before my birth. He suggested we see what was going on with my throat and hands. So I was hypnotized for the second time. When asked what was in my throat and in my hands, I said it was my father's penis. I was a small child; we were in the outhouse and my father was drunk. He used me for oral sex. I had buried that experience deep within myself for thirty-four years.

Coming out from under the hypnosis was one of the most powerful spiritual experiences of my life. I was not alone. The whole group was with me. It was raining outside: it felt like a cleansing rain to me. "I feel like a sacrificial lamb," I said. The footprints prayer came to mind about the man who dreamed he was walking along the beach with God. His life passed before him and as he looked back at the footprints in the sand, he noticed that at the most difficult times in his life there were only one set of footprints. He asked God why he had abandoned him during the worst times of his life. God replied, "My precious, precious child, I love you and I would never leave you. During your times of trial and suffering, when you saw only one set of footprints, it was then that I carried you."

I too had thought God had abandoned me, during all those times that I know now I was being carried. I realized that to be who I am today, there must be a presence of good in the universe for me. One night during the clinic experience, I had a spiritual experience that is hard to describe, but the message I received and was able to internalize was "I am in God and God is in me."

I feel better knowing about the incest than not knowing. This knowledge helped me to make sense of many different physical reactions. For example: whenever I attempted any kind of public speaking, whether it was a five-minute introduction or speaking in a class, I had a tremendous fear of being found out. Yet I did not even know I had a secret. My throat has always been the most vulnerable part of my body. Any time I was under stress, I would either get a sore throat or my glands would swell. That is no longer true. I had always hated French kissing (and not because it was a sin). I felt a strong physical reaction whenever anyone was in my face, feeling as if I was going to be suffocated. I am grateful that that is no longer true.

The secrets buried deep within me created other barriers as well. Knowing about the incest has opened me to all kinds of possibilities. At a retreat three years after the clinic experience, I wrote in my journal a dialogue with the incest. In the meditation before my journal-writing, I received an image representing the idea that God is in me and I am in God. This sustained me as I wrote this dialogue:

> Me: Okay, Incest. It's you and me here in this room. I am trying to be open to what more you have to teach me. I am grateful for the spiritual and sexual awakening that came along with remembering the incest.
>
> Incest: You have done well with seeking support and with sharing your experience, strength and hope. As you know its not something you will be done with in three years. It's been three years now, right?
>
> Me: I guess so. It's gone fast. It seems I have to keep learning over and over that I'm not done yet. I'm glad I also learned to get on with life—and not stay stuck in the grieving. Help me let go of my self-consciousness about this dialogue. I imagine someone listening to this, and I feel inhibited.
>
> Incest: It is not an easy subject to speak out about. You have been courageous before, and you will be again. Just as I am a teacher for you, you must share what you learn in order to keep it. (The silence must be broken.)
>
> Me: Help me recall what I've learned.
>
> Incest: Well, first, the spiritual awakening that came with remembering—the recognition that a power greater than you is and always has been with you. The greater power that got you through your childhood. Second, your realization that you are part of that greater power just as that greater power is part of you. We are not

separate entities. And you are beginning to grasp the significance of this in empowering people, especially those who have a difficult time identifying with the old-white-man-in-the-sky God. That image is useful to some people some of the time, but it also prevents all women and men of color from taking responsibility for their power and talents.

When we take responsibility for our power and talents, silence is golden. When we take responsibility for our power and talents, the silence of debilitating secrets must be broken. Out of this silence, I have learned to like myself enough to choose to spend time alone, and I have more compassion for others. I begin to understand that we never know what others have been through—we may not even know what we ourselves have been through.

Since learning of the incest, I have developed a passionate desire to explore the relationship between spirituality and sexuality. Just as my childhood image of God is insufficient for my spiritual needs as an adult, so is my understanding of sexuality and spirituality.

One year after the clinic experience, I began graduate work in theology. I focused particularly on sexuality and spirituality. As I reclaim my heritage, I relinquish the buried secrets and seek buried treasures. I am realizing the value of solitude and of an empowering understanding of sexuality and spirituality. I have discovered at least two kinds of solitude and silence: 1) the isolation of self-negation and silence of secrets that keep us separated from each other; and 2) the golden silence of listening to the God within and outside and the peaceful solitude (at-one-ness) of embracing our sexual/spiritual selves.

The writing of Joan Timmerman has been particularly helpful in my exploration of sexuality and spirituality. In *Sexuality and Spiritual Growth*, she writes: "Sexuality is the name given to the whole human person considered from the perspective of embodiment; spirituality is a name given to the whole human person considered from the perspective of orientation toward transcendent meaning."[1]

Three recent experiences in my life exemplify the integration of spirituality and sexuality.

The first is an anecdote involving my son. When he was learning to ride his bike, he tipped over and gashed his knee. As I cleaned him up and tears streamed down his face, he said, "I like myself." I said, "I'm glad you like yourself," and he said, "I love myself." It took me thirty-seven years to learn to say nice things to myself when I was in pain, and he knew to do this at five.

Earlier this year I attended a program in which we were given a simple, yet powerful exercise called, "Being With." During the activity, I got in touch with the deep sadness over the life and death of my father. I was able to break another silence and express my love for him. I asked a dear friend to "stand in" for my Dad and listen to me for him. I cried about the times I missed being with him. I cried about the times I wanted him to die. And I said, "I know you love me; now I need to know that you know I love you." I received the reassurance I needed.

My third experience has been writing this paper with the intention of expressing myself as a sexual and spiritual human being. All of us have experiences or opportunities that call us out of victimization into being more fully alive.

These six years have not been easy, but I know they would have been worse without the daily, weekly and annual times of solitude that saw me through a job change, a divorce, several moves, and the death of my father. Today, I can say I am happy with my life. I am healthy. I have a good relationship with my son. I have good friends and meaningful work. Periodically I have to remind myself that I am not finished yet; I have not arrived. I would like to have a better relationship with my family of origin—my mother and my sister in particular. And although I have come to enjoy my solo dancing, I would like to have a dance partner. I want a relationship where we will be guardians of each other's solitude.

1. Joan H. Timmerman, *Sexuality and Spiritual Growth* (New York: Crossroad, 1992), 25.

Solo Dancing on the Spiral Quest

Christina Baldwin

There was a night in my life recently when I understood what solitude is again. It was a night of falling stars, in August, when the earth annually passes through a meteor shower. A friend and I, in northern Minnesota, hiked up a cliff, propped ourselves against a slab of exposed Canadian shield, and waited for the light show to begin.

The Canadian shield is the oldest exposed rock on the planet: 3.5 billion years old. Pushed up and left by the glacial shift, this is the mother of all stones. Twenty minutes after resting my spine on this hard bed, my body was trembling with energy as the rock of the planet and the rocks of the cosmos signalled each other. I vibrated in the force field between them, electrified by earth and stars, all my personal molecules whirling. I felt on the verge of dissolving into energy, dissolving into the not-self, which is unity, which is oneness, which is solitude. I felt realigned and made again aware that what hurls through the space between the stars is the same stuff that hurls through the spaces within the atoms of myself.

This "stuff," I believe, is what we call solitude: the basic element of the universe, the non-matter out of which all matter is made, the source of creation. Certainly in my own life, experiences of solitude have been the source of creation, and, since I am a molecular creature, I assume my patterns are set, to a large degree, by universal patterns. We may call this core material by other terms: Creator, God, sacred, soul, *prana*, Mother, Father, goddess. We don't know its real name: we know only our experience of it.

We engage the experience of solitude in order to touch our innermost being at the point where the self touches the Divine. Whatever path we take, in whatever tradition we pray, we know somehow that the universal adage is true: God *is* silence. Sacred presence occurs beyond words in moments of awe and unity, and most often when the self is dipped deeply in solitude: alone on a rockface, alone in meditation, watching the breath and sensing the lives of the cells. And it has always been so; human beings need solitude, solitude brings us into relationship with the divine mystery and allows us to heal by reuniting our splintered-off selves with Unity.

The most basic evidence we have of the shift from animal awareness to human consciousness indicates the need to experience relationship to the Divine: to ritualize moments of awesome solitude; to paint the cave walls of Lascaux, which can be entered only by crawling a half mile through an umbilical tunnel into the earth; to place the boulders of Stonehenge in a circle beneath the sky; to create rituals that invite the members of the tribe to participate in singular and communal acts of questioning. For to question is to assume relationship, to assume the possibility of response. In solitude we ask, "What is humanity that Thou art mindful of us?" And in the reverberations of our question we are put in touch again with our inner selves and our mystery.

Touching mystery needs to be interwoven into our daily activities, integrated into our lives as they are. For me, that means finding solitude on the fly, catching it in small pockets of time, choosing to be still and opening myself to stillness, even for a few moments.

I am a pacer. I circle the pages of my journal, the unread books stacked by the bed, the computer humming quietly in the office corner. I go up and down the hallways of my house getting another cup of tea, checking the laundry, answering the phone, until, finally, someone in my family asks in exasperation, "What *are* you doing?"

And I turn to them in amazement and say, "I'm meditating, can't you tell?" However we struggle to make space for solitude, however we practice it, somehow we must learn this solo dance, for we cannot become one with the One, until we become one with our self.

Much of the spiritual journey is traveled in the mind, and mind-travel occurs through consciousness. Consciousness is the ability to live life and think about it at the same time. We live life on three levels that comprise consciousness: the life of the actor, the life of the observer, and the life of the storyteller. I call these aspects: the walker, the watcher, and the writer. The walker is the self who lives through daily events. The watcher is the self who observes these events and reflects upon them. The writer is the self who synthesizes action and reflection and creates story, oral and written. Story creates meaning. Story orders and reorders events and makes things fit into patterns we can understand, or can, at least, contemplate. I lived through my moment on the rock face, reflected and wrote about it, and now have integrated it into my life story as an event accorded meaning within the larger context of the rest of the story I carry about myself.

This enriched, threefold consciousness allows us to hold ordinary moments close to our hearts and to put experience into words so that the heart and mind can interact to perceive reality.

Medical scientists have now discovered sympathetic nerve endings that run from the heart to the brain stem and have observed that when something happens, these sympathetic nerves are activated in the chest *before* they are activated in the brain. We are upside-down in our thinking in this culture: we think the intellect knows first, and we're wrong. Experience enters us at the heart *chakra*, at the sacred heart, and then informs the mind. And then the mind messes around with the heart's knowledge until we have no idea what the heart originally experienced and communicated. It is at this point of confusion we desperately need to enter solitude, so the mind may still itself, and the heart can speak clearly again in its quiet voice.

The consciousness that emerges from the heart-mind dialogue is a total commitment. The decision to wake up to ourselves and the journey, to call upon ourselves to be present, is a decision to go all the way with life. We will be unalterably changed by this willingness, and so must approach consciousness with trembling, with great respect. Consciousness grows, and it requires that we grow with it.

Our moment may happen quietly, a meditative thought that acknowledges: "I know . . . and I know that I know," which is perhaps the modern equivalent of Descartes' declaration, "*Je pense donc je suis.*" ("I think therefore I am"). Or consciousness may happen dramatically, as in that emblazoned awakening when Annie Sullivan shoved Helen Keller's hand into the cold pump water and spelled furiously into her palm, "Water. W-A-T-E-R. It's a word, Helen, it means something!" And the light dawned, and the great consciousness that was Helen Keller came into the world.

Although solitude is a highly intuitive and often unformed experience, it may be described as four stages of relationship:

- choosing to be reflective in our daily lives,
- removing ourselves from routine in order to see what emerges,
- carrying solitude within ourselves when we return to the world,
- experiencing solitude as direct interaction with the Sacred.

The first level of this spiral journey is *choosing to be reflective in our daily lives*. Reflection creates solitude. To notice, to slow down, to be mindful of what we are doing is a revolutionary act in a culture in which life in the fast lane is considered the only lane. We are constantly invited to speed up and told that speed is the essence of productivity.

In light of this cultural pressure, an interesting experiment was conducted not long ago in France. A car company stationed two automobiles at the town limits of Charleville, on the northeast border near Belgium, and instructed the drivers to cut diagonally across the country, following a specified route, to travel as quickly as possible to Bayonne, a town at the southwestern border near Spain. One car was to travel at five to ten kilometers over the speed limit, run the yellow lights, cut corners and cut time, as much as it safely could. The other car was to go exactly the speed limit, stop at the yellow lights, follow the letter of the law, stop for pedestrians, and so forth. Crossing an entire country, the speeding car arrived in Bayonne, twenty minutes ahead of the slower car!

We are not saving time in the fast lane. What happens is that we get hypnotized by the illusion of speed, instead of enticed by solitude. We are all vaguely hypnotized much of the time anyway; we choose to be enthralled by the river of the mind, by the flow of traffic.

Catching yourself in the act of living is the basic stage of awakening. As you practice noticing, you become more and more mindful of action. You are sitting at your desk drinking a cup of tea. Do you taste it? Do you give thanks for it? Do you invite it to nourish you? Do you think about where the plants grew that made this tea, how the leaves were dried and who dried them, how the leaves got into a tea bag and into a store and into your cupboard and into your cup? What will happen to that used-up tea bag, and what is your relationship to this entire process? We cannot do everything mindfully and get very much done, at least in the ways most of us define efficiency and productivity, but we can practice turning mindfulness, like a lantern, on different, small aspects of our habitual routines.

The mind is capable of divided attention and automatic action; mindfulness teaches us to watch the mind making choices and decisions at a level we may not have observed before. When I wanted to lose a certain amount of weight that had accumulated since my fortieth birthday, I decided to become mindful of the decisions I was making about food and to change my relationship to what and why I was eating. Before putting anything in my mouth, I stopped and asked my body a series of questions designed to help me be mindful of my activity: Is this morsel *exactly* what you want? What do you think eating it will do for you? Is your hunger physical or spiritual? What other choices could you make? Is there a longing underneath the reach for food?

Out of the process of mindfulness and choice-making we are able to develop authentic commitment, which is very different from dieting. We are able to commit ourselves to noticing that sacred presence is available to us in our daily lives, and to integrating that experience. Life becomes ritual, instead of habit. And one consistent ritual is to dip into solitude, to bring ourselves into a spiritual framework for daily living.

The next level of solitude is *removing ourselves from routine in order to see what emerges.* The way we do that is through meditation, retreat, study—any reflective activity that interrupts habit. When you're stuck in a spiral, to change all aspects of the spin, you need only to change one thing. This is true about tornadoes, which is why their path is so unpredictable; they are constantly being influenced by obstacles of air and ground and whirled in a different trajectory. It is a phenomenon more safely observed by spinning a top or a gyroscope. Tapping the toy, just a little bit, anywhere as it turns, will make it spin off on a new course. So, one way we grow in the spiral journey is to allow ourselves to be tapped and nudged by reflective experience. When we hit against our routine, the altered spin gives us new perspective.

It does not matter how you meditate, retreat, or seek your quest; what matters is that you do something to take you out of routine, that you go in search of your relationship to the sacred. Ram Dass tells a wonderful story about this. He lectures extensively and was talking one night to a large audience comprised mostly of aging hippies, but there was one very old woman sitting near the front, watching him intently. She appeared very conventional, perhaps someone more likely to be playing church bingo than listening to an esoteric lecture, but she kept nodding enthusiastically at everything Ram Dass said. Feeling challenged, he got wilder and wilder, but no matter how far-fetched his stories, she kept nodding in agreement. He never reached a point where she seemed shocked or ready to disagree.

At the end of the evening they met in the crowd and Ram Dass asked her, "Madame, since you seem to be so familiar with the concepts I was discussing, I have to ask you how you came across this philosophy of life."

The woman leaned forward and whispered into his ear, "I crochet."

The third level is *the ability to carry solitude within ourselves when we return to the world*. Coming out of meditation or retreat, we often speak of inner calm, quiet, insight, and peace as conditions we wish to maintain. What has happened in retreat is that the ego has relaxed, relinquished its attempts to manage our lives and let the soul-self receive inner guidance.

Now, the egotistical world—the world of business and commerce and politics and getting things done—doesn't believe that the soul is very good at any of this. So conflict is created inside ourselves. We have the tendency to become dichotomous, to use the ego to drive our lives through the week, and to take out the soul on Sundays or in rare moments of solitude when we aren't trying to do anything practical. The challenge, of course, is to integrate, to interweave the ego and the soul so that our weekly living is imbued with spirit, and we are not cut off from all that we are.

Solitude introduces us to the soul. In silence, we discover that someone else resides in us who is not ego. As the richness of the soul-self emerges through our testing of relationship, we begin a long process of shifting our self-concept from the ego to the soul. This shift is not an abandonment of ego: our dual nature is an essential aspect of our humanity. Even the great prophets and teachers have struggled with this dichotomy of ego and soul, and it is in the tension that choice takes on its meaning. Even Jesus, praying in the Garden of Gethsemane, experiences this tension. His ego tries to negotiate a way out of the destiny his soul has long ago accepted. In the prayer, "Let this cup pass from me . . ." He asks God, "Do I really have to do this? Are you sure this is the only way?" At the same time, the transcendent Christ-energy has accepted, surrendered, and is already at Heaven's gate.

For ordinary mortals, the choice is perhaps not as extreme, but it is the same tension: the ego cannot understand how the workaday world and the world of the spiritual heart can co-exist. The ego tries to decide what is reality and to make all experience fit within the prescription. More and more, in the spiral journey, these definitions break down. We are confused, or at least part of us is confused, and our confusion and our clarity are housed together in the same body, mind, and heart.

The ego is designed to preserve the body-self: to protect the littleness, the ordinariness, the physical comforts of our lives. The soul is designed to commune with the not-self, to know God, to disregard physical comfort and ordinary concerns, to reach for larger understandings of our life's purposes. Through practices of solitude, the soul increasingly attaches itself to the mystery of God. The soul's quest puts the ego in great tension; we need our ordinary lives, and we need our spiritual lives. It's as though the Self is a car with two drivers. The ego is good for getting us around the neighborhood, but the soul needs to drive the long distance. The ego needs to come along on the spiritual trip, but it can't drive anymore. The soul needs to drive. We are practicing, in the most practical and elemental fashion, transcendence.

I had the opportunity to think about transcendence in the juxtaposition in my life between the death of one friend and the pregnancy of another. When my friend Lynne had cancer, there were many times when the most healing thing I could do was just lay hands on her. As I did this, I became very aware of the energy emanating from her. As she prepared herself to separate from the body, the energy in her body shifted. Her vibration changed, became transcendent, impersonal, atomic radiation itself.

A year after Lynne's death, my friend Deborah was forty and pregnant. The pregnancy was problematic and she was exhausted. A few days before labor, we spent an afternoon during which I just held her feet and massaged them while we talked. Her energy had that same transcendent quality. After she had delivered a healthy baby girl, I wondered whether the vibration that exists at the gate into life and the gate into death is the same. Perhaps in those moments when we are closest to life or death, when we open ourselves to the mystery, we all vibrate with this atomic energy.

What I believe happens to us at the vibrational level of solitude is that we begin to understand that we are feeling a relationship through energy. The human being and the Sacred vibrate together. Over time, we learn to endure this vibration with greater and greater understanding. We develop a sort of spiritual stamina and allow this energy to interact, communicate and consciously influence us. Through this point of energized communication, we bring the will of God into the world; we become God's hands and feet and voices.

Vibrational interaction allows us to move to *directly experiencing the Sacred*. These moments of direct experience are deeply mystical and hard to explain. They belong to the region of the heart's knowledge, beneath the mind's created language. We know them in ourselves viscerally, energetically, by admitting to profound stillness, ecstasy, unity, oneness. The religious word most often used to explain this experience is *grace*.

In unity, we touch life with child-like wonder, step into it and forget to stay separate, forget to stay grown-up, forget to stay in the busyness of the mind. The heart simply blasts open. We have moments of unity with other people, children, even strangers. We have moments of unity with nature, with autumn leaves and spring buds, with sunrises and snowfall. We allow ourselves to become one with whatever is awesome within the present moment. And out of these moments, we recreate our lives, integrating spiritual experience and accepting the mysterious, unfathomable, yet discernible, shape of reality.

The more deeply we experience solitude, the more we need this recreation of life, because the less we can assume we understand. We see that reality is a collective hunch, a pastiche made up by families, by religion, by ethnic background, education and cultural systems in which people, over time, have agreed to agree. This chair is a chair because we all know it is a chair, call it a chair, treat it as a chair, and have an "I-chair" relationship to it. Solitude opens us to the atomic, the energetic level again. Solitude allows us to reconsider reality: to look at the chair and see the wood, to imagine the tree, to plant the seedling, to walk in the forest, to hold the spinning molecules in our hands. We find the world.

This is not a New Age experience; this is the thread of mysticism that has been woven into human consciousness since the dawning. In her book, *Practical Mysticism*, English poet and novelist Evelyn Underhill, wrote:

> If the doors of perception were cleansed . . . everything would appear to man as it is—Infinite. But the doors of perception are hung with the cobwebs of thought, prejudice, cowardice, sloth. Eternity is with us, inviting our contemplation perpetually, but we are too frightened, lazy and suspicious to respond: too arrogant to still our thought and let divine sensation have its way. It needs industry and goodwill if we would make that transition: for the process involves a veritable spring-cleaning of the soul, a turning-out and rearrangement of our mental furniture, a wide opening of closed windows, that the notes of the wild birds beyond our garden may come to us fully charged with wonder and freshness, and drown with their music the Gramophone within. Those who do this, discover that they have lived in a stuffy world, whilst their inheritance was a world of morning-glory; where every titmouse is a celestial messenger, and every thrusting bud is charged with the full significance of life.[1]

When we accept a mystical relationship with life and with the mystery of God, we discover that all our perceptions are up for review: Who am I? What is my real potential? What is the true nature of the world? How might I lead my life differently, and in so doing make the world different around me? Our explanations disappear. We need solitude again, to sit with the chaos of the mind and ask for guidance. We pray, "Give me words and understanding, O Mystery. I can no longer spin the story of myself. I await the directions and guidance I need for going on."

Practiced at this level of awareness, solitude is a dream state, and we proceed from the dream outward. Sometimes the dream is accompanied by story, a line of words that can float at this level, and sometimes there is only presence: the energy of the universe, which is love.

Near the end of his life, when Gandhi was aware that the principles of nonviolence he had tried to instill in the hearts of his country-people were not going to resolve centuries of conflict between the Hindus and the Moslems, an interviewer asked him, "What then do you still believe?"

Gandhi replied, "I believe only one thing . . . that love *is* God."

No matter how the ego fights and avoids it, you and I seek solitude because that is where love lives, and we are drawn in. We are drawn to this point where love/God can touch us and clean us out and empty the junk and allow us to be filled with grace. We agree to engage—with Spirit—in mental house-cleaning, to make ourselves ready and available and able to act.

In my combined careers as a teacher and writer, I have probably reached through my words between 50,000 and 100,000 people. Because of the nature of my writing and teaching, I know that these people have in common a willingness to seek the inner life. This is a community of pilgrims, journeying on a huge collective pilgrimage. In my personal teaching experience, approximately seventy percent of these seekers are women: women who have been keeping journals and reading widely. Women who are going through therapy, recovery, and spiritual guidance. Women who are healing, questioning, changing, and empowering themselves. These women are asking themselves, me, and others, "What do I do with this spiritual experience? I am not the woman I was meant to be. I have lived that life and let it go. My children are grown. My marriage is stable—or gone. I don't know what to do, but I have a deep urgency to do *something*. I have ten, fifteen, twenty years of energy left and I want to impact the world. I see that the world needs me, but I'm struggling to get at it effectively. I want to fulfill my life."

I believe we are at the point at which we can integrate and combine solitude and activism. We are, individually and collectively, moving from isolation to community, from introspection to action, from victimization to power. We exit the cycle of personal healing and enter the cycle of spiritual obligation.

While you and I have been on our journeys to heal from the individual, traumatic circumstances of our lives, the rain forests have been cut, the hole in the ozone has widened, the children have continued to die of dehydration and starvation, and decisions are being made by our supposed leaders that will take centuries to repair, if they are repairable at all. Spiritual obligation is the decision to respond to these conditions with active and informed love: to extend the healing we have experienced in our personal lives toward the life of the planet. For I believe if we can heal the atom of ourselves, then we are capable of healing the rest of the atoms, which are our neighbors, our countries, our planet.

We can take our theological insights and empower them in action. We can cycle back through the first stage of solitude and bring our insights into our lives; cycle through the second stage and bring our insights out of retreat; cycle through the third stage and integrate solitude so that it lives within us; and we can stand in the crisis of the times, in the fourth stage of solitude, willing to re-create the world so that there is room for love, for mystery, for the tit-mouse of God to bring us word of what we are to do. And then we can, must, do it.

Solo dancing is necessary, and so is our great communal dance, to rise up and accept the challenges that the soul calls forth within us. What solitude will ask next of me, I do not know, you do not know. Our responsibility is to the act of silence itself: to still ourselves, to become the question that is open to reply.

1. Evelyn Underhill, *Practical Mysticism* (Columbus, Ohio: Ariel [E. P. Dutton & Co.], 1914), 40-41.

9.

Power and Ambiguity

We as women need to examine our fear of power. There is a comforting complacency that accompanies powerlessness. Power carries responsibility. Inertia can be hard to overcome.

CHERYL MALONEY
Theological Insights, September 21, 1990

The Power of Ambiguity

Kay Vander Vort

I approach the topic of ambiguity with a certain sense of inadequacy. So much of what I am about to explore I am still trying to live or understand myself. No point of arrival exists, of which I am aware in my own life, except the desire to "wake up and embrace the struggle."

I imagine myself walking into a dense, thick fog where no clear, sharp images and colors emerge, only a cloudy haze. The haze reminds me of my mid-life effort to look up phone numbers in the directory without my reading glasses. I see some hazards on this journey to ambiguity because not seeing clearly will make the way scary and ominous. Most of the road markers will be question marks with a few exclamation marks and almost no periods. This journey is a solitary one that I must travel at my own pace.

My first step is to define the word "ambiguity": a statement, act, or attitude capable of two or more contradictory interpretations. Something ambiguous is difficult to comprehend, distinguish or classify. While groping around for my own clear understanding, I found myself reaching for *Roget's Thesaurus* where I stumbled upon some associations that first shocked me, but then confirmed the historical roots of many of our problems with church, society and family.

The thesaurus referred me to "uncertainty" as a synonym for "ambiguity." As I read down the list of affiliated words, such as "perplexity," "dilemma," and "quandary," my eyes slid over to the next column headed "certainty," the opposite of "uncertainty." Here I found words like "gospel," "scripture," "church," "pope," "court of final appeal," "positiveness," "dogmatism," "know-all," "bigot," "no question," "not a shadow of a doubt." These are the definitions we have inherited. We recall phrases like "the gospel truth," and "I swear by the church," both phrases meaning unchanging or unquestionable. In the past, perfection (a goal to be attained) has been equated with the static and unchanging. But as I reflect on my own life, I realize that, more and more, my experiences and their meaning present themselves to me as ambiguous.

I grew up a dedicated rule-keeper. Living as an only child in the confusion of an alcoholic home, I had to have some things on which I could count. As a little girl, I loved the Roman Catholic Church in my Iowa town: the organ music and incense, the mysterious Latin phrases, the people huddled together on their knees in the long rows of pews, always jam-packed at the eleven o'clock Sunday Mass. I found comfort in the structure of the church. The rules were very clear, and I could count on them. However, now when I look back, I remember some ambiguous moments.

One poignant memory was the annual parochial school recruitment. That Sunday, the gentle, though somewhat remote, pastor tapped into some real passion in his homily and chastised all parents who did not send their children to the parish school, as well as all children who did not go there. I went to public school. I still remember vividly the feeling I had as I scrunched down in the pew hiding from the shame— of me, of my parents who were not *good* Catholics.

I have heard stories in and out of church settings where the loving and caring authority somehow turned judgmental and angry. What is important for me now, in recalling these stories and recognizing their power in my development, is to let the message of ambiguity speak to me. For example, could the church be both good and bad for me?

I have learned that ambiguities increase with life experience. These days when I come home from an R-rated movie like *Fatal Attraction*, with its explicit sex, I can hardly remember that other world in which I lived where I used to dutifully and somewhat regularly confess (at about eleven or twelve years of age) that I had committed adultery because I had looked overlong at some "impure" pictures in *Life* magazine. And what's more, the priest who heard my confession never said anything to me about my "adulterous" conduct even though in that same confession I almost always gave clues to my tender age by confessing that "I disobeyed my mother and father six times." This same church that was so concerned about my sexuality gave me some very conflicting and confusing messages. The model for holy family life was one perfect child, born without pain to a virgin who lived with a husband who never consummated the marriage. What did that do for me in my adult years, as I grappled with the church's teachings on birth control? How could I truly love my husband and four children and continue to have every sexual act open to the possibility of pregnancy? I knew after my fourth child that I had reached my level of incompetence, mentally, emotionally, psychologically, and physically. Could a loving church and God ask so much from me?

My children while they were growing up gave me wonderful theological reflections on ambiguity. For example, "If our team prays to win and the other team prays to win, how will God answer?" Or, "If God loves us, how come he lets tornadoes come?" After years of living with teenagers, my faith in the value of ambiguity got stronger. Logic and clarity did not always work. "Yes, there is no one else using the car tonight, but no, you can't have it!" "Yes, I trust you, but no, you can't stay out all night." And again in the area of sexuality, I, who had lived by the rules, found that I had mothered children who *questioned* the rules and had the audacity to ask questions like, "What's really wrong with living together before you're married if you're going to get married anyhow?"

One of my most recent experiences of ambiguity was with a group of long-time friends. We had enjoyed a lingering lunch together catching up on news of our common friends. One woman told us of a mutual friend, formerly a nun, who was now living with a man. We had a lively discussion about the morality of this with comments ranging from "Good for her!" to "I can't believe she could do something like that!" Finally one woman blurted out in obvious pain, "Aren't there any absolutes anymore?"

For the most part we have not been prepared or encouraged to understand our lives in terms of ambiguity. Instead we have been taught to live and think in dualisms such as good or evil and saint or sinner. Growing up, I believed that "holiness" necessitated these qualities: non-emotional (no feelings), nonsexual, praying ceaselessly, alone with God, barely tolerating the body, ignoring what to eat or wear. The preferred life was a relinquishment of the world and its pleasures as well as the body and its pleasures. That was the model for saintliness or holiness. But I actually heard more about the opposite of holiness which is sinfulness.

I learned the seven deadly sins—pride, gluttony, lust, avarice, sloth, envy, and anger—the Ten Commandments, the stain of original sin, the difference between mortal and venial sins, and the lure of worldly pleasures. What I did not hear much about was the place in between perfection and damnation. That middle place, the fulcrum of a teeter-totter. Sure that I could not rise up to the holy side of the teeter-totter and scared to death that I would slide down to the evil side, I resignedly thought of myself as lukewarm, not capable of heroic living. What I never considered until just recently, with suggestions from the writings of Carl Jung, is that the holy place is the middle place, the place where I struggle to balance the tension between the good and the evil in me, where I acknowledge the capacity to be both saint and sinner, realizing that if I go out over to one side too far, I will come crashing down. That's my fulcrum theology.

The teeter-totter image works with other dualisms as well. For example, body and soul. We have received an overwhelmingly negative view of the human body from Christian history, which suggested that the soul developed at the expense of the body. The body's needs were best repressed, denied, ignored, subjugated to the higher, nobler realms of the soul. The body/soul split, which put concerns of the soul above or superior to concerns of the body, seems to be haunting us these days, particularly women. We are constantly struggling with body image and succumb to diet fads, weight-watching, calorie-counting, and a multitude of eating disorders. Very few women like (let alone love) their own bodies.

Recently I have discovered in talking to other women that we have all had an experience of looking back at an earlier photograph of ourselves and realizing that our bodies looked better (thinner, usually) than we remembered feeling at that time. Many of us realized that we could hardly remember a time when we were satisfied with the way our bodies looked. Today we are increasingly aware that we cannot live ignoring either body or soul. We are learning that we need medical care to be whole human beings and that changes in the habits and conditions of our bodies open our souls to greater insight. Contrary to what we may have learned, Christianity affirms the human body by the doctrines of creation, incarnation, and resurrection.

The universe can teach us to live with ambiguity. Nature's mind is not oppositional. Day and night, hill and valley, summer and winter, are different phases of reality that show us how to live in ambiguity.

Part of our problem is that we live cut off in our cities from the world of nature. We live isolated and insulated from the lessons of nature.

A few years ago I had an opportunity to get out of my protective, safe environment. I went to Africa on a photographic safari. The experience was a breakthrough for me. I was overwhelmed with the magnitude of God. The variety of animals (most of whom I had seen only in zoos) were within arm's reach, standing free, eating, running, playing, staring at us as we clicked our cameras. I was high on God.

Then one morning our driver pointed out a lost young zebra running frantically, within the huge herd of zebras, obviously confused and panicked. He told us that she had been separated from her mother. Whether her mother had fallen prey to the lions we did not know, but the reality was that no other mother would come forth and this young zebra would run until she dropped or was caught by a lion spying an easy catch for supper. Later that same day, we came upon another scene of terror. A female hyena, having snubbed the sexual advances of several males, was suddenly viciously attacked by at least six hyenas of her group. She was forced into a culvert and, though I could not look, I am sure she was killed by her own kin. I was face to face with the inherent violence of nature, survival of the fittest, and I was mad at God. My nice image of a loving God did not square with the harsh facts. I had to look at the concrete data that the Creator of life and beauty had also allowed for death and disaster.

If we are lucky at all, we will find ourselves at some point confronted with a life situation that shatters our neatly held assumptions. In this breakthrough situation, certitude flies out the window along with our former goals, values, directions, and answers. Ambiguity replaces certainty. If we are to grow, we must invite ambiguity in. Wholeness and integration do not come if we repress consciousness, ignore awareness, and deny the good in opposing values. If we deny, repress, or suppress the creative power within the ambiguity, we deny the new being we are destined to be.

In my own journey into ambiguity I have been guided, prodded, jarred by becoming aware of my dreams. I found that, while I could control my conscious thoughts with some success, my unconscious kept bubbling up in dreams that challenged me. An example: Several years ago, I spent a year as an intern in the pastoral ministry program at The College of St. Catherine. During that time I had a memorable dream; in fact, the dream occurred the night after my mid-year evaluation:

> I am all alone in the Pastoral Ministry office on second floor Whitby.
> I go out into the deserted hall and a little old woman dressed in

"ethnic" clothes is obviously looking for help. She asks me for help, and I look all around, trying to think of whom I can get to help her. My feeling is, "I'm not in charge here." Then the woman slides open the glass door of a trophy case and out comes a very crumpled little old man—very, very small. He is her husband. The woman is a little more forceful and angry now about her husband needing help. I think to myself, "They'll never make it through all the channels and departments here—the red tape. I'll have to help them." So I begin to organize their care, trying to prioritize what to do first as I know they need physical, emotional, and mental help.

As I worked with this dream, I realized that my instinctual gut-level self (symbolized by the ethnic woman) was trying to pull out the masculine strength, which, though very small and weak, was nevertheless in a trophy case—obviously a "prize." And most of all, the message was that my ego self, myself in the dream, was the one to do it. Although I was held, housed, and supported by the institution, I ultimately had to seek my own path and I needed my whole self, body, mind, and spirit.

Living with the topic of ambiguity has led me to five new realizations, which I share not as conclusions but as catalysts for others. My first realization is that if meaning is ambiguous, then we are not condemned to live out an unfortunate sense of meaning on which we settled early in life. There is always an alternative aspect to consider. For example, as a young woman who chose to be wife and mother as my primary vocation, I believed wholeheartedly for many years that my success as a woman depended on how my children turned out. It was a breakthrough for me and my children when I finally realized that it was simply not true that my success as a woman was dependent on my children's achievements. It was a great relief and freedom for all of us.

The second realization is that the success of the patriarchal system has been to make unthinkable the possibility of alternatives. One of the first questions in the *Baltimore Catechism*, a major training tool for young Roman Catholic children in the past, was "Why did God make me?" The answer, "God made me to know, love, and serve him in this world, in order to live forever happily in the next," was unambiguous. As long as I regarded it as *the* answer or an answerable question, I was unable to pose the question for myself, "Why *did* God make me?" The real truth is that I was taught both the question and answer long before I even cared.

The third realization is this: women who have been socialized and trained to doubt self can, with healing and encouragement and support, transform that self-doubt into tolerance for ambiguity, a gift sorely needed in our culture. I have a very fresh example of that. After writing the first draft of this paper, I decided to read it to my son who is in law school. He told me that I should never begin from a position of weakness. If you remember, I began by saying, "I approach the topic of ambiguity with a certain sense of inadequacy." However, I set about changing the introduction to make it begin from a position of strength. Self-doubt had the upper hand, though I still liked my earlier beginning because it had come from my heart. As I sat with it, I decided not to change it so readily and at least to get another opinion from a woman, my friend. She supported me in staying with my first beginning. I defied the "rules" for powerful writing and have allowed myself to trust my inner truth.

My fourth realization is that tolerance for ambiguity is the antidote for fundamentalism—religious or any other kind. If we admit that there is not just one path to God, that the Bible and other religious formulations carry the influence of the cultures that shaped them, that revelation is not static but in process, we will have a receptive attitude.

My fifth realization is that the search for meaning is open-ended. This does not eliminate the search, but encourages it. An old German story about the hands of God illustrates this. God had never really finished making humans and thus had never seen a finished person. God determined to send her right hand into the world to take human form. That hand held all truth. But she was not fully satisfied with what she learned from this one hand. So she continues to send her left hand into the world. That hand is empty; it holds the space for search, for pilgrimage. Since humans still are unfinished, they must begin with the left hand. One cannot receive the fullness of the right except through the pilgrimage of the left.[1]

At some point in our lives, we have to decide that everything matters or nothing does. If we decide to pick and choose what parts of life are real and loving and exclude everything that hurts or is more than we can understand, then we are going to live a very different life than if we embrace all of life and find out what life is about by living it. Can we celebrate the diversity and live at the fulcrum place? That balance of tensions is well-described by T. S. Eliot as "the still point of the turning world, neither flesh not fleshless, neither from nor towards, at the still point—there the dance is!"

---

1. This is a composite of two German stories from Rilke and Lessing told by the theologian John S. Dunne in *The Way of All the Earth* (New York, Macmillan Inc., 1972), 93-95.

The Ambiguity of Power

Anne E. Patrick

> To live by faith means to accept one's own power, always partial
> and finite, always power-in-relation, but nonetheless real. . . . The
> opposite of faith is despair, hopelessness, acquiescence to one's
> powerlessness, and refusal to act as a responsible agent in moral
> struggle.[1]
>
> —Beverly Wildung Harrison

Do women want power? How eager are we for leadership roles,
for positions of authority? How willing are we to use the power of
influence by speaking out, by writing for publication, by direct and
sustained confrontation with others?

Women are, at best, ambivalent about power, and there are good
reasons for this. For one thing, power is ambiguous. We can distinguish
the negative power of coercion from the positive power of energy, possibility, and influence. We can visualize, on the one hand, the power of
Simon Legree with the whip and, on the other, the power of the battery
that brings a car to life in fifteen degrees below zero or the power in a
friendship that energizes us in ways we had not imagined possible.

Contemporary theologians have probed these ambiguities. Carter
Heyward wants to leave behind views of power based on competi-
tiveness (where power is something that either one or the other party
has but never both at once) in favor of a power of mutual relationship.[2]
Bernard Loomer contrasts "unilateral power," which produces effects

without mutuality in the process, and "relational power," or the "capacity both to influence others and to be influenced by others"; in other words, the "capacity to sustain a mutually internal relationship."[3]

Although such distinctions are useful, they can be misleading if we expect that under the conditions of finitude the good type of power will be one hundred percent realizable whenever we wish it. This unrealistic expectation can paralyze us with an idealism that refuses to act in imperfect situations, thereby removing us from politics, the "art of compromise." This matter of perfectionism is related to a second reason why we are ambivalent about power; this has to do with our socialization as females. Since girlhood we have been schooled in precisely those traits of character that make it difficult for us to claim our power.

Valerie Saiving recognized this problem as early as 1960. She argued that traditional notions of sin and virtue reflect experiences typical of males who enjoy power in society.[4] For such men, pride has rightly been identified as a most harmful inclination, with temptation to sensual indulgence at others' expense also a recurrent danger. Thus, exhortations to cultivate humility and self-sacrifice are appropriate for them. But to universalize this analysis, and especially to apply it to women, whose social location is ordinarily quite different, is to exacerbate the moral problems most women face. Given the disparate social experiences of the two sexes, the *temptations* of women are different from those of men. Instead of pride being the greatest danger, for most women the chief temptation has been the opposite—to fail to have a centered self, to yield up responsibility for identity and actions to other persons and environmental factors. Whereas men of privilege are tempted to *abuse their power*, women (and men of oppressed groups) tend to *abdicate their possibilities for using power properly* for the sake of approval and security. What women in patriarchal society need are not exhortations to humility and self-sacrifice, but encouragement to value ourselves and our possibilities. We need to risk criticism and even failure for the sake of accomplishing things that are good and reasonably attainable. We also need new models for virtue and new stories involving what I call the "pretty good" use of power, in contrast to the unattainable "perfectly good" use of power—in other words, stories where women act when some of the evidence is unavailable and are willing to undertake a reasonable risk of losing present good for the sake of a greater good that is likely to come.

This moral growth entails moving from a style of being responsible that is predominantly passive to one that includes creativity and risk-taking. Passive responsibility involves being dutiful and living up to the demands of our roles. Creative responsibility looks beyond the predefined role descriptions of the "good Catholic laywoman" or the "good sister" and sees a myriad of possibilities for action, indeed a world in need of transformation. Creative responsibility involves being conscientious in promoting good through realistic appraisal of the likely consequences of a decision. It requires willingness to act without absolute assurance of being right. Instead of relying entirely on others' formulas for behavior, we can do our own interpreting of what is happening and our own analysis of how our actions might contribute to the betterment of life for ourselves and our neighbors. This by no means rules out benefiting from the wisdom of others, but it does rule out abdicating our judgment to other authorities. We risk being mistaken and criticized, but the rewards are high: an enhanced self-esteem and a sense of being a full adult participant in life rather than a minor who is only marginally involved in shaping self.

Both types of responsibility have their usefulness, like the white and black keys on a piano. The problem is that our socialization has equipped us too well for the one and very poorly for the other. Women and men alike have been damaged by forms of moral training that minimize the agent's role in interpreting obligations and balancing those that are in conflict. Women, however, face special problems as the result of our socialization that typically fosters passivity and stifles growth toward exercising power and creative responsibility.

This socialization sometimes sets women on a tragic, misguided quest for innocence, which confuses goodness with not taking action in ambiguous circumstances. Playing into this dynamic is a spirituality that lacks trust in God's daily forgiveness and in God's supportive presence in our process of making choices in situations where innocence is hardly possible, given the ambiguities of life situations. Jesus seems to have known about such ambiguities. Why else would he have stressed the need for daily forgiveness in the prayer he taught his disciples? But in subsequent centuries of ecclesiastical management of divine forgiveness the ready accessibility of forgiveness has been forgotten by many Catholics. What we need above all is a sense of God's enabling power and presence, along with a reconstituted vision of what authentic moral responsibility requires.

The theological argument I have sketched draws on insights from other fields, including sociology, philosophy, and psychology. I shall discuss some findings from these disciplines on women's socialization and the use of power.

In her 1983 volume, *The Political Integration of Women,* sociologist Virginia Sapiro describes her efforts to discover why, more than sixty years after women gained the vote in this country, we are still quite marginal to political life. For her research, Sapiro administered questionnaires to school girls and to adult women and compared the results. The striking difference was that the girls felt very knowledgeable and self-confident about politics and their potential for affecting the world. But the women had lost this sense of capability and power. Why? The hypothesis that provided the best answer to this question was that the *responsibilities* associated with women's adult roles contribute directly to the political marginality of women. Sapiro identifies "privatization" as a key culprit in this regressive process. Privatization involves the mindset that women are intended to center our lives on traditionally "feminine" concerns, mainly domestic and nurturing ones, with the result that we are perceived, and we see ourselves, as not really capable of effective action on broader matters.

Clearly Sapiro is talking about passive responsibility when she says such things as, ". . . adult norms become internalized in a desire to be a 'good parent,' 'good wife,' 'good worker,' or 'good citizen.' Adult responsibility means knowing what is expected of one and fulfilling that expectation."[5] She finds that efforts to conform to the ideals associated with "feminine" roles—efforts to be docile, passive, supportive of men—result in low self-esteem and low estimates of women's power. These efforts keep us from being full participants in our democratic society. In short, the orientations fostered by being a "responsible" woman in the passive sense "form a clear picture of the acquiescent member of a political community."[6] And so women wait. We wait for a liturgy that nourishes our spirits; we wait for a meaningful work situation or supportive living environment; we wait for justice in the church and in the world.

The image of waiting is also prominent in Madonna Kolbenschlag's 1979 book, *Kiss Sleeping Beauty Goodbye,* which examines several fairy tales as "parables" of women's socialization and shows how cultural myths can dwarf our spiritual and ethical capacities.[7] In a chapter called "Sleeping Beauty at Seventeen," Kolbenschlag describes how young women are conditioned to wait for that magic kiss that will awaken them to existence. In this state of waiting, they allow their own spiritual powers to atrophy. Typical of this attitude of waiting is what Kolbenschlag calls "the desire to live for another." She writes:

> This role will school [the young woman] in self-forgetfulness, service and sacrifice, in nurturing rather than initiating behaviors. Above

all, it will teach her to "sleep"—to wait, forever if necessary, for the expected other who will make her life meaningful and fulfilled. She will give up everything when the expected one comes, even the right of creating her own self. Whether it is a husband, a religion or a revolution, she is ready to live outside of herself, to abdicate responsibility for herself in favor of something or someone else.[8]

Women who have been drugged by our cultural myths, Kolbenschlag says, will seek fulfillment through others and, while waiting for this vicarious fulfillment, will regard themselves as persons "that things happen to, not as [persons] who make them happen."[9]

Carol Gilligan makes a similar point in her study of psychological theory and women's development, *In a Different Voice*. She speaks of the perceived conflict between "selfishness" and "responsibility" that leads in many instances to the "mysterious disappearance of the female self in adolescence," when an underground world is mapped out and "kept secret because it is branded by others as selfish and wrong."[10] Influenced by cultural pressures to epitomize "the morality of self-sacrifice," a woman may live and suffer under the mistaken assumption that "she is responsible for the actions of others while others are responsible for the choices she makes."[11] Such women will usually be very responsible in the passive sense. They will pour vast amounts of energy into conforming to others' expectations, but in a deeper sense they remain morally asleep.

The poignancy of this situation for any woman is expressed by the character Monica in *The Three Marias: New Portuguese Letters*: "In the end, what difference can my absence from this world make to you, if all I gave you was my absence from myself. . . ."[12] All in all, Kolbenschlag's investigation of feminine myths and models leads to a finding remarkably similar to that of Virginia Sapiro:

> The passivity and privatization of women in our society are the most serious obstacles to their own autonomy and personal growth, and also to the transformation and redemption of the entire social structure.[13]

This research leaves us with the obvious question: How are we going to overcome this socialization to passivity that keeps us from really claiming our power? To begin to address this question, let me suggest three factors that are required for our moral empowerment: (1) we need to understand and accept these ambiguities involved in responsible action in a world where few choices are without risks or negative consequences; (2) we need a support system that both challenges and nurtures us; (3) we need models of self-critical decision-making in which the ambiguities of power are taken into account.

As an example of such a model, consider the following case, which Yale theologian Margaret Farley analyzed in 1982 at the convention of the Catholic Theological Society of America. In a talk entitled, "Power and Powerlessness: A Case in Point," Farley described the then recent conflict between the Vatican and the Religious Sisters of Mercy of the Union over the issue of tubal ligation. Note the clear reasoning that went into the decision of the leaders of the community to submit to a Vatican directive to withdraw a letter they had sent to hospital administrators inviting dialogue on whether tubal ligations should be available in Mercy hospitals.

> The decision to forego a public position of dissent was not made because of a new belief in the teaching of the magisterium (on the issue of tubal ligation) or out of religious obedience to a disciplinary command. This does not mean that the Sisters of Mercy accept no fundamental authority in the Church, or that they see themselves in regard to their life and ministry as only autonomous agents in the Church, not subject to the Church and its legitimate authority in an important sense. It does mean that in this case they could not find the teaching of the magisterium persuasive and, in fact, interpreted the demands of the magisterium as an attempt to use juridical power to settle a question of truth. Perhaps even more importantly, they perceived the demand for continuation of a policy which they were convinced was unjustly injurious to other persons (patients in their hospitals) as contradictory to the overall obligation of the Sisters of Mercy (in fidelity and obedience to God and the Church) to carry on a ministry of healing. In other words, without special further justification, these specific demands by church officials entailed doing evil.[14]

Why then did these women decline to take a public position in opposition to the magisterium? After attending to three competing values—community, ministry, and truth—they judged that in this instance silence and submission were necessary to preserve the religious community and its ministry. And so they *accepted the evil entailed* in "material cooperation" with a problematic Vatican directive and hoped that their decision would lead ultimately to greater good for the Church.

Farley describes the decision in terms of a relatively adequate choice that must continue to be scrutinized:

> The decision of the Sisters of Mercy must still be reviewed and critiqued by those within the Community and without. The answer to

the question, "Why did this group of women agree to be silenced?" seems . . . to be this: "In order that theirs and other voices may ultimately prevail." The danger, of course, is that the silence will grow, and that power in the church will be more and more isolated, especially from the experience of women. But this story is unfinished.[15]

These words show that the fact that knowledge is limited need not paralyze our powers of judgment, but rather can allow for decisions to be made in trust and hope, with a conscience consoled by the assurance that God's mercy will compensate for the ambiguity entailed. It is too soon to know whether the community leaders' choice was better than the alternative in terms of its effects, but I find the decision-making process a model in terms of the awareness the women brought to the process and their willingness to tolerate the ambiguities that seemed necessary to endure.

The task I see ahead, then, involves continually challenging ourselves to be responsible in modes that *include ourselves* among those deserving of our care and that refuse to relinquish the task of discerning our obligations and acting according to what we judge God is asking of us. To move thus to the level of creative responsibility will inevitably lead to clashes with patriarchal authority, for to leave behind passive responsibility is to stop living up to the Victorian ideal of women as "angels in the house." Sad to say, those who judge by patriarchal stereotypes have only one other category in which to put women who are not angels, namely that of monsters. Thus we should not be surprised when our judiciously thought-through decisions evoke responses all out of proportion to what we have said or done. Response is not to the words or deeds themselves so much as to monstrous image of female insubordination. Women are not supposed to be assertive or autonomous or powerful, and those who do not behave like Snow White will inevitably be linked with the Wicked Witch of the West.

As long as *we* have other categories for interpreting ourselves besides angels and monsters, this aspect of existence under patriarchy need not trouble us unduly. But knowing the stereotypes that we face is part of what is necessary for a realistic assessment of the likely consequences of what we decide to say and do.

I conclude with another positive model, an example of a woman acting with power under ambiguous circumstances in Washington, D.C., that city of politics and power. I have in mind Theresa Kane's decision to respond to repeated refusals for private conversations with Pope John Paul II by using the occasion of a formal welcome to convey a message she deemed urgent for him to hear. After greeting the Pontiff at the beginning of a prayer service at the National Shrine of the Immaculate Conception in October 1979, Kane, then the president of the Leadership Conference of Women Religious, went on to say:

> I call upon you to listen with compassion and to hear the call of women who comprise half of humankind. . . . The church in its struggle to be faithful to its call for reverence and dignity for all persons must respond by providing the possibility of women as persons being included in all ministries of our church.[17]

Kane's action was unexpected and controversial, but it epitomized creative responsibility in the way it balanced conflicting values within limited circumstances. She had the duty to express welcome and respect; she had the obligation to represent the injustices experienced by those who had chosen her as leader. Both concerns found their way into the course she finally elected, and, to my mind, she succeeded in "speaking the truth in love," providing a new image of what goodness for a Catholic woman can mean, of what the responsible use of power in ambiguous circumstances can look like.

1. Beverly Wildung Harrison, *Our Right to Choose* (Boston: Beacon Press, 1983), 92-93.

2. Carter Heyward, *Our Passion for Justice: Images of Power, Sexuality, and Liberation* (New York: Pilgrim Press, 1984), 116.

3. Bernard Loomer, "Two Kinds of Power," *Criterion* 15 (Winter 1976): 20, 23.

4. Valerie Saiving, "The Human Situation: A Feminine View," in *Womanspirit Rising*, eds. Carol Christ and Judith Plaskow (New York: Harper and Row, 1979), 25-42.

5. Virginia Sapiro, *The Political Integration of Women: Roles, Socialization, and Politics* (Urbana: University of Illinois, 1983), 47.

6. Ibid., 106.

7. Madonna Kolbenschlag, *Kiss Sleeping Beauty Goodbye: Breaking the Spell of Feminine Myths and Models* (New York: Bantam Books, 1981), 3.

8. Ibid., 10.

9. Ibid., 12.

10. Carol Gilligan, *In a Different Voice: Psychological Theory and Women's Development* (Cambridge: Harvard University Press, 1982), 51.

11. Ibid., 82.

12. As quoted in Kolbenschlag, 27.

13. Sapiro, 78.

14. Margaret Farley, "Power and Powerlessness: A Case in Point," *Proceedings of the Catholic Theological Society of America* 37 (1982): 117.

15. Ibid., 119.

16. Theresa Kane, quoted in *The Washington Post*, 8 October 1979, A-25.

10.

Manifestations of the Divine Feminine

*We are the most human when we are out of control,
which is to say, when we are engrossed, engaged
and enfolded in holy mystery.*

KATHERINE MCLAUGHLIN, CSJ
Theological Insights, October 14, 1988

The Embodied Feminine

Mary Pinney Erickson

"Feminincarnation" is the integration of the feminine, the body, and the sacred in one individual life in communion with all life. For me, this integration has been an on-going struggle because I am a woman who was not raised to be a woman. I was raised—in my own family and in the Catholic church—by the patriarchy. When I first realized this, I thought perhaps I had been raised to be a man. On further reflection, however, I found that I was actually raised to be a neuter. In neuter there is no power and no identity.

I learned very well to live my neuterness. I stuffed any feelings that might have distinguished me. I ran from my body, never experiencing the joy of my soul being one with my body. I hid from my gifts. I grew up as I was taught and I became, not a woman with ideas and feelings and breasts and goals and yearnings, but a good little child. I knew all the rules, and I knew that keeping them would keep me safe. What I did not know was that trying to keep *all* the rules would either kill me or drive me insane.

Fortunately for me, the Sacred Feminine One burst into my life before I was completely lost. She burst through in the only way she could to draw my attention away from the patriarchal ideal for females: she came to me in a dream, *disguised as a man!* So now, several years later, I—who was taught to fear my body, to be disgusted with flesh, to look on the female body, especially, as sinful and the source of most evil—*I* am the one called upon to write about feminincarnation! What an incredible sense of irony she has! And so deeply does she yearn to be a part of our lives that she works for our attention in any outrageous way she has to!

I do not write from an extensive knowledge *about* her, but from intense experiences of her, both in my own life and in the lives of others. When I first began to write of these images of the Divine Feminine, I found myself writing about *my* images. After talking with other women, I know these images are not mine but *ours*.

There are, I believe, three essential elements in feminincarnation: our bodies, our images of the Divine Feminine, and the birthing process which unites the first two. We must begin with our own bodies.

How can we dare to speak of an embodied feminine if we cannot love our own bodies, if we cannot experience the union of our own spirits with our own flesh? How can we expect to understand or live incarnation if we cannot understand or live with the bodies in which the Holy Spirit is enfleshed? We *are* hungering for a return of the Feminine God to consciousness. We are hungering to death. In fact, some of us are hungering for it so much that we are literally, physically starving ourselves to death. Some of us are filling ourselves with substitutes which cannot satisfy our hunger. In this process we binge and purge; we develop addictions to various substances or behaviors; we form dependent relationships, thus destroying ourselves with a living death. We hide our hunger for the Divine Feminine deep within our numbed bodies. We hope to silence the hunger.

But the hunger goes on because we do not know how to satisfy it. No one has ever taught us what this hunger is for and we are too frightened to face the hunger alone. The blessing we are given now is that we no longer have to face our hunger alone. As we share our awareness of this hunger, we have each other on whom to lean. We also have experiences and images of deep satisfaction to share with one another.

Oddly enough, the Christian tradition has included images for what we need, in words like "indwelling" and "incarnation." We have used these words ourselves, but we hardly understood or accepted what we were really saying. We cannot honestly speak of incarnation or of the feminine without using words which make us uncomfortable or embarrassed: words like earthy, emotional, chaotic, passionate, enfleshed. And we cannot relate to the feminine side of God until we are willing to explore the meaning of these words in spite of our uncomfortableness and embarrassment. We need to learn how to listen and relate *beyond* the embarrassment in order to reach the Divine

Feminine calling to us from the other side of these feelings.

Although many feminine images of God exist, I will focus on just three aspects of this feminine God who seems to create such uncomfortableness in us. These are aspects that I have come to know, to respect, and to love. They are the Chaotic, the Compassionate, and the Passionate.

When the Divine Feminine first appeared in my dream disguised as a man, she cold-bloodedly gunned down a room full of card-playing men who were gambling with my life. Suppressed by the patriarchy for centuries, she can often be imaged as The Wrathful, Vengeful Feminine—her face drained of color, fire in her eyes, wild hair, her voice shrieking in the anguish of the banshees. She is then the Goddess of Destruction and Chaos who *demands* the sacrifice of all that is comfortable and probably stagnant in our lives. She demands a death; not a simple death which leads to a quick resurrection, as when we speak of the death-and-resurrection of Christ as though it were a single word describing a quick and easy passage. No. She represents the missing piece, the part between the death and the resurrection. She is the Goddess of the Entombment. (Even Christ spent time in the cold, dark tomb.) She demands not just a death but a rotting, a decaying of all we have been. We can know somewhere deep within ourselves that this rotting is necessary and will become the mulch, the stinking fertilizer for our new growth and our new life beyond the darkness. But this awareness does not help us while she is here demanding her due. All we know then is the pain and the rage.

We fear her because of the depth of her pain and the power of her rage. We know she is carrying these feelings for our sakes and that she is here to teach us how to sink into this darkness. This is when we need to accept that to rage is a holy act, to scream is a prayer, and to weep is a baptism. This is her way, a way of opening us to the divine force of ever-changing life energy within us. She abhors complacency. She desires to connect us with our own feminine power which is dynamic, not static.

But we have a choice. We can choose to experience her consciously in our own way or unconsciously in any way she chooses. If we choose not to learn her lessons and try to bottle up her energy within our bodies where it has been stored forever, we fight a traumatic battle. Distorted by our fear, her energy bursts forth from our guts, wreaking destruction all around us. Ignoring her turns us into the Medusas we do not wish to become. Then, we turn our relationships, our families, our careers, our health into stone.

Her energy is powerful, and she wants us to be conscious of her power. But in our fear we cannot see that she is offering us a way into our own creative energy, that she is leading us into being just who it is we were created to be, not who we were *raised* to be, but who we were *created* to be. She is not about destruction only for the sake of destruction, even though it sometimes seems that way. She is about destroying the old to make fertilizer for the new. There is not just light at the end of her dark, spiraling tunnel. There are rainbow explosions of union with divine light. But, to get to these explosions, we must be willing to submit to the rotting, even when we have no sense of the eventual outcome, maybe *especially* when we have no sense of the outcome. This is how we honor her presence within us. If we are willing to walk around in our own shit for a while, we will soon see that everywhere we step, new life shoots up in the fertilized fields around us.

I know this is true because I have lived it in the cyclic pattern of life which she creates. I have accompanied a dear friend through this death. I see it happening now to another. It is agonizing. It is also life-giving, because the sacred feminine one is not only chaotic, she is also compassionate.

When we feel as if the puzzles of our lives have just been tossed into the air and we have no idea where the pieces will land, she is with us. When it seems as though everything around us has been swept into a sandstorm and the landscape has disappeared and nothing is familiar anymore, she is the one who sets up a tent for us, an oasis in which we can rest. When everything around us is in motion and it seems that we will never find peace again, she is the one who reassures us and cradles us in the *midst* of the motion and the chaos that our lives have become. When we finally turn around to face the wounds from our past and the emptiness that was never filled, she is there returning to the past with us, transforming it for us, loving us through it. She is Nurturer, Comforter, Mother-Breast flowing with warm milk. She treats us with infinite tenderness.

She is not afraid of our tears. She knows how to hold our pain gently, to stroke us softly, and she asks only that we *feel*. She does not need words from us to describe the pain. She experiences our pain fully and asks us to do the same. However, she does not ask us to feel it alone, but in the comfort of her arms. We can hardly conceive of the possibility of comfort in the very midst of chaos. But this is who she is.

We can hardly believe that there is someone who can be with us in pain and not try to cheer us up or talk us out of it or distract us from it. We are surprised that she invites us into our hurt, that she accepts both the joy and the pain of life equally. She wants to teach us the same acceptance. She wants us to learn how to hold the tension of the opposites in life long enough for our new life to crystallize beyond the tension. She loves us wherever we are on the cycle of getting it together and letting it fall apart. She reassures us that there is enough love in the world to sustain us, that we do not need to grasp for love, to cling to it desperately before it slips away, or to cry out for it unsatisfied for the rest of our lives. From her we learn not to believe the lies that we cannot endure and that we will never be loved enough. For, while her chaos is devastating, her compassion is extravagant.

A third image of her is the passionate feminine. She is about pleasure, earthiness, groundedness, relatedness, sexuality. She is the one who invites us to feminincarnation. If we are honest with ourselves, we know that we experience the gnawing, aching hunger for union with the beloved, the intense yearning to be desired by the Sacred One whom we desire. We yearn for union. We are made for this. Whether we are male or female, we are drawn into love. She is the one who draws us. She creates the fire of desire in us, puts us in touch with our hunger for the one who is other. And she asks us to ground this experience in our bodies, to feel it physically. She does not accept a "head-trip" relationship with the divine. She asks us to turn ourselves over completely to our desire. She asks us to listen to our bodies as they cry out for the divine presence. She asks us to yield our lives over to our hearts, and this, *after* she demonstrates to us that we have no control over our hearts.

Oh, how we fear this! "Let go? My God, what are you asking of us? Allow the spirit of love to guide our steps? Do you know the incredible trouble we could get ourselves into?"

She laughs at our turmoil and turns up the heat. So we have to struggle with how our prayer got to be so sensual and how our sexuality got to be such fervent prayer. She ridicules our unquestioned assumptions that some parts of our bodies are less holy than others and then she focuses our attention on our genitals.

We begin to think we are going crazy as we struggle within the corsets of dualistic morality that have kept us safe but which have painfully bound our bodies for so long. We begin to feel our own passionate energy. We begin to suffer from lower back pain. The sexual images in our dreams become more frequent and more insistent. Any person who represents "other" to us becomes suddenly very attractive. We find ourselves needing touch more than ever. Then we are really frightened and have no recourse but to couple our prayer for mercy and relief with an equally heartfelt prayer to remain open to her call.

She calls us, then, to move beyond our fear into an acceptance and a celebration of our own eroticism. She wants to free us to recognize and name the yearnings within us. She wants us to come sexually alive and we have to learn the true asceticism of touch: when to give ourselves over to abandon, when to practice restraint, how to ground our sexuality in her love. Her call is not simple. She can demand celibacy of us as easily as she can demand union. She accepts only an authentic response from our bodies. She wants us to learn how to be passionately alive, how to use our passion to love creatively. She challenges our so-called belief in the incarnation by demanding that we cherish our own flesh, that we listen to her presence in our own flesh, that we communicate our love for her and for one another with our own flesh.

We were created with this deep hunger for union because the one who created us in her image hungers for union with us, desires to be desired by us with an even greater intensity than we can imagine! This union is for the sake of our wholeness, our holiness. It means accepting the dark, shadowy parts of ourselves. She invites us into a spirituality which includes personal responsibility, public sharing, and authentic interaction as a corrective to the patriarchal demands on women to be submissive, sacrificing, and invisible.

How are we giving birth to this feminine side of God in the world today? The sacred feminine is coming to birth in the world because of our willingness to say "Yes" to the whole process of birthing her: to being penetrated, conceiving, carrying, laboring, birthing, and nurturing her. This birthing process is rooted in love. We must learn to discern how to be open only to love. The divine feminine does not force herself on us. She waits to penetrate and fill us until we offer ourselves to her.

To be truly penetrated, we have to be present *here* and *now*, and we have to be open to Love in spite of our fears or our training to be otherwise. This means accepting whole-heartedly that incarnation means the flesh-taking of God. Some of us were taught as children that we were temples of the Holy Spirit and that we needed to care for our temples. But somehow that did not mean caring for our bodies. It meant taking care of some hidden inner place that was not physical. But, it *is* our bodies which are the temples! It is *in* our bodies that we worship. We raise our hearts to God joyfully and easily. Some of us, as we become more comfortable with our bodies, can raise our arms to God joyfully and not self-consciously. Will there ever come a time when we can raise our crotches to God joyfully?

Being penetrated means experiencing the fire of the divine *in our bodies*. Not just parts of our bodies, but our whole bodies, from the tips of our toes to the crowns of our heads without bypassing certain parts. Yes, this process is embarrassing and creates an intense struggle within us. We question. We scream. We plead. This is part of the birthing because she wants us to be honest, to feel the struggle, to name it, to hold the tension between the anguish and the ecstasy. We who were raised to follow all the rules are now being challenged to break almost all of them for love of the divine feminine. Allowing ourselves to be penetrated is nothing short of terrifying and wonderful, all at the same time. Allowing our desires for wholeness and union to surface, to consume us, to lead us into the unknown, we are led into a time of holy pregnancy.

This pregnancy is a time for grounding ourselves in our bodies. This means recognizing our bodies' need to be loved, touched, cared for, and treated with gentleness and compassion because of the deprivation these bodies have suffered. We can honor the body for her willingness to carry the burden of our darkness; we can love her for enduring for our sakes hatred and degradation from others as well as from within ourselves. We can validate her pain born in the dualistic time when the mental had supremacy over the physical.

Grounding ourselves in our bodies also means taking responsibility for proper nourishment during this time of pregnancy. This nourishment includes allowing ourselves to feel and share our feelings honestly. This nourishment includes relating to and caring for, not only the earth within us but also, the earth around us. It means identifying with the sacredness of the dark as well as the sacredness of the light.

To nourish ourselves in this time of pregnancy means trusting our own feminine wisdom, intuition, and experience and honoring this feminine in ritual, story, poem, song, art. It means recognizing the lies we were taught about our bodies and about the feminine, rooting out those which tell us that we are responsible for everyone else's sexuality and that our bodies are dangerous and evil. We can replace these lies with truth. We can also nourish ourselves by choosing a midwife, someone who knows what this experience is like and who can love and support us through it. (After we have been through this birthing, we can also choose to midwife others.) And perhaps most importantly, we can nurture ourselves through this pregnancy by being *gentle* and patient with ourselves, with our beloved goddess, and with a long and sometimes slow process.

This nurturing of ourselves through the pregnancy process leads us to an intense experience of labor and birth. This is a time when we must trust the silence within. It is a time of almost painful interior awareness and a time to depend on the wisdom of the midwives among us. This is a time when we move from being women of the patriarchy to being women who honor the feminine—physically, intellectually, psychologically, aesthetically, and spiritually. We do give birth to new life, the new life of the feminine spirit within us and among us.

Giving birth to the embodied feminine means that we birth women, not neuters. We birth women filled with energy of the sacred feminine. We become conscious, healthy, delighted women who are present to our God, our selves, our bodies, our companions, our world. We understand and live the cycles of our lives. Once we have birthed the divine feminine, we pray with our bodies, love with our bodies, minister with our bodies.

Birthing the divine feminine means that we are different kinds of partners than we expected to be when we married. It means that we maintain our own identities and work *with* our spouses, not *for* them. It means that we bring all of ourselves into our primary relationships, and we fight, if necessary, for the intimacy we need, even if that means raging fiercely or abandoning ourselves to ecstacy (both experiences the patriarchy has taught us to fear). It also means that we are free to open ourselves to receive love from those who truly love us, in the ways in which they need to give it.

Birthing the divine feminine means that we are different kinds of mothers than the media and the institutions around us believe in and support. We interact authentically with our children, expressing the full range of our emotions. We share our excitement in being who we are called to be. We teach them respect for the feminine and willingness to experience the feminine in themselves, whether they are male or female children. We love them through crises even when society labels and discards them. And we demand that they (and not we) pay the consequences for their behavior.

Birthing the divine feminine means that we are different kinds of sisters and friends than we were taught by the patriarchy to be. We love other women openly, desire to know them deeply, seek them out frequently, open our hearts to them trustingly, sit with them in their pain, and encourage their growth as they encourage ours. We are drawn instinctively to the developing feminine in men. We celebrate their feminine development without denigrating their (or our) healthy masculine qualities. We become aware of and sensitive to enfleshed visions of our goddess all around us in our homes, neighborhoods, workplaces, schools, and worshipping communities.

Birthing the divine feminine means being different kinds of believers than we were raised to become. It means believing in our own priesthood. It means questioning, challenging, speaking up, offering our gifts because we are called to be prophets whether or not religious institutions recognize or invite our charisms. It means calling the church to justice within its own ranks. It means working for peace because our hearts yearn for it. It means living an incarnational spirituality. And it means that even our images for the masculine side of God become more sensual, more intimate, and more balanced.

Birthing the divine feminine means that we are different kinds of ministers than the patriarchal church can yet envision or accept and different kinds of disciples than any people who have ever lived discipleship before us. We know our own woundedness and our own strength, and we use both. We determine the focus for our ministry by considering both who we are and what the needs are. We are not intimidated when we do not have it all together because we know the source of our ministry. We minister passionately and physically. We work for the one who loves us even when we know we may not see the results of our toil and we do this because we know that what we do is for *her* people.

We need to nurture our infant, embodied feminine. This is not easy to do. When we choose to break free from the collective stereotypes and the rules of society to be the individuals we were created to be, we suffer from the backlash. The people around us, reacting in fear or anger, try to get us to conform, to return to being the "nice" people we used to be. When we do not conform, we are sometimes called selfish, uppity, evil, emasculating, unfeminine, bitch, and worse. This is painful and frightening. It brings up our anger. In spite of this pressure, we can still continue to believe we are pregnant with the possibility of the divine feminine, even when other people tell us we are just "full of it."

But the exterior backlash is often nothing compared to our own interior backlash. We have internalized the collective ideals. We are full of inner voices that represent these ideals and from which we need to separate. These voices tell us in a thousand ways that we are wrong, that no one will support us, that we are no good, that we are to blame for everyone else's problems. They attack us when we are tired or weak. We need the courage to tell these interior voices to shut up. We need the courage to continue in spite of the tension they create in us.

We need the courage to ask one another for support when we need it. She who is sacred calls us into relationship. She asks us to *receive* her. But we always have a choice. We can choose to focus on the up-tightness we may feel when the feminine is equated with receptivity. But, this very same tension and denial may be exactly what keeps us from opening to receive her. We can refuse to receive. We can close ourselves off, tighten up even more. We can choose to be touched only exteriorly, the touch never penetrating our skin. We can choose to taste just barely as food rushes through us, bland or over-salted and over-sugared. We can choose to smell only occasionally, perhaps when we encounter tar or skunk or the better portion of someone else's cologne bottle. We can choose to hear just enough so that it does not register and does not trigger a response or ignite a conversational connection. We can choose to see only fuzzy, half-remembered faces and images. We can choose not to receive.

We can block it all out, holding everything, everyone, every experience at bay—every feeling locked tightly inside; everything else locked tightly out. We can build impenetrable barriers. We can live out of fear and a false feminine. Or, we can choose to receive our feminine god. We can choose to listen to her call as she says to us: "I want your hearts to be open to receive eros, your mouths to receive and give my words . . . my songs, your minds to receive understandings far beyond the ones you were taught, your bodies to receive your souls, your souls to receive the fullness of the divine presence, your lives to receive all of the possibilities. Openness is not always easy," she tells us. "Parts of you seem to be welded shut. So, it will take a great upheaval to open these parts. But if you are willing to continue, we *will* accomplish the complete opening, the complete flowering of who you are."

When we choose to hear her call, our bodies tremble and cry in response. We lose control. We feel our pain and also our deepest joy. We are then out here on the fringes of the known world, trying to speak about how *round* the earth is. People tell us we're crazy, that the world is flat; has always been flat, and will always *be* flat, and, if we keep going, we will surely fall off the edge. But nothing will stop us now because we have seen the curved horizon. We have discovered the God who is feminine. We have learned that we were not an after-thought in the creation of the world. We have found some sisters and some brothers with whom to travel, and we know in our bodies that we are accepting the invitation to have life and have it more abundantly, here and now, when we choose to embody the feminine.

Seeing the Feminine Face of God

Joan H. Timmerman

In the account of his TV interview with Joseph Campbell, Bill Moyers tells this story: "In Japan for an international conference on religion, Campbell overheard another American delegate, a social philosopher from New York, say to a Shinto priest, 'We've been to a good many ceremonies and have seen quite a few of your shrines. But I don't get your ideology. I don't get your theology.' The Japanese paused as though in deep thought and then slowly shook his head. 'I think we don't have theology,' he said, 'We dance.'"[1]

But we, as women doing theology, walk in two worlds; we theologize and we dance. Some of us are learning to theologize while we dance; others are learning to dance while we do theology. Seeking the feminine face of God is a common theme for our reflection. In my reflection I aim to make the feminine face of God perceptible to experience. The other side of the task is to make theological sense of our experiences. Ultimately we all need to do both.

We are, in this process, trying to make faith-sense of experience and at the same time to make experiential sense of faith. My personal study of theology has been a quest to find an overall context for the meaning and purpose of life within which to locate all our ordinary experiences and to interrelate them. The most challenging feature of my study continues to be checking such a vision of life against each new experience as it arises. This is an approach shared by many theologians, not just feminists.

To identify the feminine face of God in our world, we need to ask: How do we know the divine in our world at all? Then, what clues alert us to epiphanies or manifestations of the divine? I will identify two characteristics of alleged manifestations of the divine that may give us confidence that what we seek (the feminine face of God) has really found us! I want to be clear that I am not referring here to a feminine part of the divine (the nurturer as opposed to the initiator) but the whole divine in female as well as male images. We can also ask: How do we experience the reality of God's feminine face through our bodies, our lives, our world? My method is to look at the tradition—biblical, theological and ecclesiastical—and ask my experience to critique it, expand it, and uncover its potential.

How do we know the divine in our world? This is a very important question. In light of the present tendency of feminism, as of most liberation movements, we are extremely critical of the given conceptual world but uncritical, almost to the point of blindness, with regard to its own presuppositions. The current debate among feminist thinkers is between two camps: those who want women's experience included and those who see it as normative. Those who say women's perspectives must be incorporated into our definitions of humanity evaluate the male norm as too narrow and attempt to transform it by the inclusion of the fruits of women's experience and reflection. Those who say women's perspective is the desirable norm attempt to set up female experience and modes of knowing as the new and true norm. Since we are organic beings, connected to the past and sharing a world with others of different gender and culture, the first position seems more compelling to me.

We can know the divine in our world by listening to the inside of our experience. We hear the possible word of a loving Voice at the heart of the universe. Karl Rahner defines human being as one who listens for intimations of the divine. These intimations have been perceived, wondered over, prayed about, and recovered in ritual form. They have come in private joy and pain as well as in the ecstasy of academic discovery and the despair of social and political tragedy. They emerge from our pondering the heart of our experience.

I find one example of such an intimation to be the Gaia hypothesis, a scientific theory developed by James Lovelock as he and others pondered the various systems by which our earth adjusts itself in terms of its temperature, its water level, its chemical proportions. He found that he could best express the reality of his findings by the analogy of a living intelligent being. Not surprisingly, the ancient name for the earth as a loving nurturing being, Gaia, was invoked. Lovelock reported in a post-publication interview that he expected scientists to react.[2] What happened, however, was that theologians responded from all parts of the world. Such enthusiastic reception may have surprised a scientist, but it is not surprising to those who know students of religion.

In fact, the intellectual process that produced the classical doctrine of God was not that far from the analysis and interpretation of experiential data that produced the Gaia hypothesis. Theology uses as its raw material the intimations of the divine that were compelling to Plato, Augustine of Hippo, Hildegard of Bingen, Artistotle, Thomas Aquinas, Julian of Norwich, and all the rest. Can it be that such intimations in our world of the reality of God are manifested in a feminine mode? Of course and increasingly.

One of the most useful and true one-liners we have from the scholastic tradition is that anything that is received is received according to the capacity of the recipient. The claim that so few intimations of the divine are received says far more about us and our conditioning than it does about God. Put another way, God can reveal to an agent only in the manner by which that agent can receive. Our ability to "receive" manifestations of the divine in female form is underdeveloped.

We can know something about God also by drawing out the implications of what God has already done. It is here that the faith-premise of the incarnation has delivered the most potential for theologizing in our century—about sacrament, about Church as human community, about the individual human being and her dignity, and about God. As Edward Schillebeeckx has said, our problem in developing an adequate language to talk about Jesus as human-divine is not our lack of knowing what it means to be divine, but more importantly, our inadequate concepts of what it means to be human.[3] As women's experience enriches our theological anthropology and moral theology, our understanding of what is meant by the self-giving of God in history, even in the traditions we already have, broadens and takes fire.

Because we are organic beings, we need our roots; we hurt ourselves when we tear off the skin of our own traditions. As I understand it, our tradition, while it is defined and limited by its past form, also includes its potential and its unimagined, undeveloped implications. Within the mystery of the incarnation lies the logical necessity that female as well as male images should mediate the totality of the divine reality. The precondition for men and women is to be able to see the finite, including the female, as the natural home of the divine.

More could be said about how we know God, confident that self-deception has not taken the place of knowledge. Awareness of presuppositions is important because it protects communication and interpretation about what is of ultimate significance in our lives. If we are aware of the human tendency to project our needs onto others and our biases onto what we see, we are less likely to fall into the trap of self-deception. To be able to communicate our own experience of God is important because without such trusted words, we would be locked in isolated individuality, and the new traditions of thought about the divine, now being developed by women, would become as much a self-serving caricature as the "male" God of the past.

One mark of the authentic encounter with the divine is that it is unutterable. Words are problematic—they conceal as well as reveal. Distrust of the power of past formulations is also one of the reasons, as hearers of the word of God, we now listen for a feminine voice of God, not because the Holy One has not been addressing us, but because the voice and the words have been so clearly and definitely men's words.

Dogmatizing about God, using masculine images and pronouns, even emphasizing the manly emotions (Yahweh does not tease or play or cry or flirt), has been uttered as if this masculine interpretation were the metaphysical truth about God; moreover, such dogmatizing is assumed to be self-evident. The assumption itself, that the revelation of God has been forever finally fixed in words, is a clue that what we have in these doctrines is not the reality of God, but an overstated image, a distortion. Fidelity to the fullness of the God behind the dominant image moves us to look more closely. And as we look for a God who confounds the unfeeling, unchanging and uninvolved concepts of God, she finds us.

A whole series of articles could be written describing alleged epiphanies of the feminine face of God. The allegations, of course, are made by those whose discoveries have, in fact, lent radiance to their lives. They cannot remove the "alleged" character objectively, for there is no clear and distinct "thing" against which to measure the allegation's authenticity. What shifts it from allegation to affirmation is the reality that *it* transforms me, lights up my life, opens me to the possibility of newness and wholeness, leads me to worship the God beyond "God."

I have been impressed recently by the recoveries being made in historical and archaeological research. Books by Gerda Lerner (*The Creation of Patriarchy*)[4] and Riane Eisler (*The Chalice and the Blade*)[5] are among the more accessible ones. The interpreters of archaeological data, which are in the form of pottery, figurines, and stone remnants, are doing something similar to what the interpreters of the myths, poetry, and historical fragments in scripture have done for us. We have the text of created nature, the texts of the Hebrew and Christian scriptures, and now the texts of other kinds of civilization, other under- standings of God, that are being recovered through study of excava- tions in Turkey and Crete.

We have learned that only one-twentieth of a mound at Catal Huyuk in Turkey has been excavated, but this digging alone has uncovered evidence of a period spanning approximately eight hundred years from about 6250 to 5400 BCE. What was found, says James Mellaart, British Museum archaeologist, after his first three sessions of work (1961-1963), "testified to an advanced religion, complete with sym- bolism and mythology; its building testified to the birth of architecture and conscious planning; its economy to advanced practices in agri- culture and stockbreeding; and its numerous imports to a flourishing trade in raw materials."[6] Only twenty-five years earlier, archaeologists still talked of Sumer as the "cradle of civilization," and this is still the prevailing impression among the general public, but we now know that there was not one cradle of civilization but several, all of them dating back millenia, earlier than previously known, to the neolithic era. And in all these places, to use the title of Merlin Stone's book, God "was a woman"![7]

These first civilizations were gynocentric—not matriarchal, but gynocentric. Strangely enough, this evidence has not generated as much interest as it would seem to warrant. Not only do the findings have artistic and religious significance, but social and cultural implica- tions. The prevailing view is that there was never a historical alterna- tive, that male dominance along with private property and slavery were all by-products of the agrarian revolution. But, in fact, this newer evi- dence suggests that equality between the sexes, and among all people, was the general norm in Neolithic cultures.

On Crete, the only high civilization where the worship of God in female form survived into historical times, tourists are to this day looking at images they do not understand. The images are called "fertility goddesses" by the tour guides, but, to my way of thinking, the term "goddess" should go the way of the terms "stewardess," "seamstress," and "seductress." What I find is an epiphany of the di- vinity. In these sacred images is documented the celebration of divine powers of regeneration. The holy and ultimate source of life is sym- bolized in sun and water, in various incarnations of Maiden, Grand- mother, Creator, Lady of the Waters and Underworld, and of divine

Mother cradling divine child. The same themes that come through Judeo-Christian scriptures are here, but broader; these images affirm the unity of all things, not just persons in their spiritual being and history, but nature as well. The interpretation of these data by theologians and the integration of this interpretation into the rest of our knowledge is long overdue. These images of the divine as female represent a text that theologians as well as archaeologists must study. When they do, we will make theological sense of an important experiential reality, new in our time.

Nature is another text where we find the feminine face of God, in the sacramental sense of the earth as God's body. Such an image implies femaleness. The image of creator as male presupposes initiating activity coming from outside. The male force enters, supplies an essential ingredient for new life. But the male remains external to the gestation process, as the metaphors of "seed" and "breath of life" illustrate. Such an image of Creator gives rise to the corresponding image of the earth as the product of God, given over to earth creatures; their exploitation and manipulation of nature, as a dead resource, follows easily. Contrast this with female imagery of creation. The new body is of the female body, in extended reciprocal relation with her. The earth can then be imaged, not as a kind of "floor" on which human activity takes place, but as full partner in the service of life.

To save our world, we need a shift in consciousness about the earth, and this shift is taking place. We now see humanity as continuing in an organic relationship to the earth, not as subject to object nor as agent to thing, but as subject to subject. The earth is a "thou" with its own dignity, deserving of our reverence. One of the lesser used criteria for the truth of our notions of God is the beauty of these notions and how they promote life and unity rather than alienation and death. When God as creator is seen as making the universe, not as artisan but as mother, her own body is the universe. As Joseph Campbell says, "the personification of creation, that is, the energy that gives birth to forms and nourishes forms is properly female."[8]

Another important illustration of the epiphanies of God in feminine form is the Virgin Mary in the Roman Catholic tradition. Once again, Campbell's expression comes to mind: in no tradition is the feminine image of God celebrated more beautifully and marvelously than in the twelfth- and thirteenth-century French cathedrals, every one of which is called *Notre Dame*. Of course, past theology provides all of the disclaimers. Mary as a historical person is not equated with God; even as *theotokos* she is not divinized. What is due to her is not worship but veneration and imitation. Insisting on these distinctions bespeaks, besides a tendency to split hairs, a preoccupation with the *distance* between the divine and the human. It is an attitude not comfortable with the human as the natural home of the divine. The symbol of Mary, with or without these disclaimers, has so outstripped the historical personage of the young woman who gave birth to Jesus, as to become, functionally, an epiphany to many people. Some cultures and temperaments more than others are able to see the face of God as feminine.

So far, these examples suggest that, while we can come to knowledge of the divine in our world, we must note that the divine is always unutterable yet seeks expression in images which are consciously understood to be partial.

Some "God, the mother" prayers sound unliberated to me, as if God were a domestic servant, if not a tamed pet. God makes her home in us and makes it impossible for us ever to feel fully at home. This aspect of God is hard to accept, but the challenging face of God is important for all to embrace, especially those who define God as love. The alternative is to be left with a God too small and a notion of love that is little more than sentimentality. The mysterious face of God is wholly manifest, not when the stereotypically feminine is added to the stereotypically masculine (the nurturer to judger, for example) but when the multivalence and richness of life is reflected in our images, symbols, and rituals of the divine.

Our moral tradition is beginning to reflect the feminine face of God. The recovery of God as unutterable mystery has had greater effect in moral theology than in any other aspect of the tradition. Seeing God as unutterable Mystery explains and combines at least two aspects of the growing edge of moral theology. One is the dialogical, non-hierarchical nature of true authority. The other is the fundamental connectedness of true authority.

The dialogical, non-hierarchical nature of true authority means that the community, as a divine and human *koinonia*, shares a common destiny and a common moral mandate. The community is enabled by the Spirit of God to live in communion with God and our fellow-people. Aspects of our recovered insight into the notion of mystery are particularly well-expressed in the drive toward wholeness that characterizes contemporary moral thought. The fact that all decisions are made in a context involving networks of relationships and connectedness to all physical reality is newly emphasized in writers such as Joseph Fuchs, Charles Curran, Beverly Harrison, Margaret Farley, Lisa Cahill, Anne Patrick, and John Mahoney. Morality is not just a matter of rules any more. Feminist emphasis on the oneness of life and the wholeness to which human beings aspire can be credited for much of this new and rich awareness. Moral theology and spirituality need no longer be separated by the gap that has yawned between them for eight hundred years. Moreover, recognition of the dialogical nature of true authority is bringing to moral theology a value for diversity. Moral thinking is persuasive when it is authoritative; it is now beginning to claim its authority through inclusivity and dialogue with people. Respecting wholeness and diversity is becoming an ideal of our time.

The second aspect of moral theology, present to many contemporary moral thinkers, is recognition of the fundamental connectedness of true authority and its ability to give life. This quality of embodied love gives authority its power to nurture, to enable, to let grow. This realization, if not a product of the women's movement, is an insight that has close affinity to women's spirituality. The product of true authority is life. What does not increase life's options should no longer be able to claim obedience. What remains important is that authority serves life, not that lesser people serve the authorities. These points could be illustrated from the moral tradition, which is not nearly so bleak as most people think. Moral thinking that is dialogical and life-giving would lead us to more, not less, liberation.

In summary, how is the feminine side of God coming to birth in our world? We have been talking not about a second conception of the sacred in competition with the traditional one, but an inseparable aspect of a single divine reality dawning on us. Augustine repeated an Alexandrine formula about the incarnation: "God became man so that man could become God." We could say that God is becoming woman so that woman can become God. Notice how much more radical and outrageous that second formulation sounds. The first statement has become a buttered phrase; it slides down without our being aware of how incredible a truth it is. If the Alexandrine formula is true, however, so is the other. Preserving our faith does not mean clinging to the formulation of it; faith is rather conceding to the Mystery.

I believe that the eyes by which the feminine face of God can be seen are being opened. Theology, as the reflection on God's presence and activity in our world and our lives, now has a chance to learn something new about God—and women—from women.

Remembering how people marveled when John XXIII spoke lovingly of other Christian bodies as brethren and when the "Decree on Ecumenism"[9] declared that Catholics could learn about God from Protestants and non-Christians, I would suggest that two such marvelous things are now happening and another is about to happen. God is manifesting the nurturing and the challenging call to humanity through women's crises and hunger for spirituality. Women are recognizing that call as from God. Men and male-defined women are about to learn something new about God!

1. Joseph Campbell with Bill Moyers, *The Power of Myth* (New York: Doubleday, 1988), xix.

2. James E. Lovelock, *Gaia: A New Look at Life on Earth* (New York: Oxford University Press, 1979).

3. Edward Schillebeeckx, *Jesus: An Experiment in Christology* (New York: Crossroad, 1981), 44.

4. Gerda Lerner, *The Creation of Patriarchy*, Women and History, volume 2 (New York: Oxford University Press, 1986).

5. Riane Eisler, *The Chalice and the Blade, Our History, Our Future* (San Francisco: Harper and Row, 1987).

6. James Mellaart, *Catal Huyuk* (New York: McGraw-Hill, 1967), 11.

7. Merlin Stone, *When God Was a Woman* (New York: Harcourt Brace Jovanovich, 1978).

8. Campbell, 181.

9. Walter M. Abbott, ed., "Decree on Ecumenism," in *The Documents of Vatican II* (New York: Guild Press, 1966), 347.

Contributors

Christina Baldwin *is the author of two books on journal writing as a transformative life tool:* One to One, Self-Understanding Through Journal Writing *and* Life's Companion: Journal Writing as a Spiritual Quest. *She teaches and lectures throughout the United States at writing conferences, retreat centers, health care and corporate centers, and colleges. A graduate of Macalester College, St. Paul, Minnesota, she holds an M.S. from Columbia Pacific University.*

Marilyn Beckstrom *serves as pastoral counselor and spiritual director at the Samaritan Center for Pastoral Counseling in Wayzata, Minnesota. An ordained clergy woman in the United Church of Christ, she is a member of the American Association of Pastoral Counselors and a licensed marriage and family therapist. She holds a B.A. degree from Bethel College, St. Paul, an M.A. in English from the University of Minnesota, and an M. Div. from United Theological Seminary of the Twin Cities where she is currently working toward a D. Min. degree.*

Margaret L. Boettcher *is director of adult spiritual enrichment and director of the junior and senior high church choir at St. Michael's parish in Stillwater, Minnesota. She holds a certificate of Pastoral Ministry and an M.A. in Theology from The College of St. Catherine as well as a Bachelor of Music from the University of Wisconsin-Madison.*

Mary Lou Judd Carpenter, *a graduate of Mount Holyoke, has also taken course work in psychology and chemical dependency, and is currently completing work toward certification in spiritual direction. Her Congregational roots inspired her diverse ministries in community leadership, Stephen Ministry, Cursillo, and pastoral care.*

Geri Giebel Chavis, *professor of English at The College of St. Catherine, is also certified as a poetry therapist. She holds a B.A. from City College of New York and M.A. and Ph.D. degrees in English from Syracuse University. In addition, she has an M.A. in counseling psychology from the University of St. Thomas, St. Paul, Minnesota. She is an active member of Adath Jeshurun Synagogue in Minneapolis.*

Mary Pinney Erickson *is both a technical writer specializing in computer software training and a graduate student in theology at The College of St. Catherine. Her bachelor's degree in psychology is from Spring Hill College in Alabama.*

Chris Franke *is an assistant professor of theology at The College of St. Catherine. She received B.A. and M.A. degrees from Marquette University and holds a Ph.D. from the Graduate Theological Union in Berkeley. Her publications include articles in* The Harvard Theological Review, Vetus Testamentum, *and* Old Testament Abstracts, *and she is currently working on a book on the prophet Isaiah.*

Elizabeth Dodson Gray *is an unordained minister with a graduate professional degree in theology from Yale Divinity School. Since 1978 she has been Coordinator of the Theological Opportunities Program at Harvard Divinity School. Her Books include* Green Paradise Lost *(1979) and* Patriarchy as a Conceptual Trap *(1982). In 1988 she edited* Sacred Dimensions of Women's Experience, *the collection that inspired the editors of* Walking in Two Worlds.

Louise O. Hiniker, *a licensed psychologist, is director of the Counseling Center at The College of St. Catherine. In addition to M.A. and M.Ed. degrees from the University of Minnesota, she is completing an M.A. in Theology from The College of St. Catherine. She is studying the relationship between psychology and theology.*

Sharon Horgan *is director of religious education and social justice at the Church of St. Luke in St. Paul. She holds a B.S. in Medical Technology from Creighton University, and from The College of St. Catherine she earned both a Certificate in Pastoral Ministry and an M.A. in Theology.*

Rose Huntley *is currently working for certification in spiritual direction at the Cenacle in Wayzata, Minnesota. She graduated from The College of St. Catherine with an English major. She is an active volunteer in church and community.*

Linda Hutchinson *works as Special Programs Coordinator at Wilder Forest, a camp and conference center near Stillwater, Minnesota. As a consultant she offers experiential training in appreciating diversity, communication, team building, and leadership. Currently completing the M.A. in Theology from The College of St. Catherine, she has a B.A. in humanities from the College of St. Benedict near St. Cloud, Minnesota.*

Eleanor Lincoln, *CSJ, a member of the Sisters of St. Joseph of Carondelet, is professor of English at The College of St. Catherine. She teaches courses in advanced writing and journalism as well as American literature and serves on several editorial boards. She has a B.S. in library science and a B.A. in English from The College of St. Catherine. Her M.A. and Ph.D. are in American Studies from the University of Minnesota. Recently she received an M.A. in Theology from The College of St. Catherine.*

Catherine Litecky, *CSJ, a Sister of St. Joseph of Carondelet, is associate professor of theology at The College of St. Catherine where her areas of special interest are scripture, ecclesiology, and biblical spirituality. Her degrees include a B.A. in chemistry from St. Catherine's, an M.S. in biochemistry from the University of Minnesota, and an M.A. in Theology from St. John's University, Collegeville.*

Sarah Hall Maney *is the author of two books of poetry about her spiritual journey,* Coloring Outside the Lines *and* Still Coloring Outside the Lines. *She manages a retail store in Wayzata, Minnesota.*

Lyn Miller, *who has a B.A. in English and theology from The College of St. Catherine, is doing graduate work in religion and literature at Harvard Divinity School. Her short story, "Fire Sermon," appeared in* Stiller's Pond: An Anthology of Midwestern Writers, *and she has given local readings from her fiction.*

Gertrud Mueller Nelson *has illustrated several books and is author of* To Dance with God: Family Ritual and Community Celebration *and* Here All Dwell Free: Stories to Heal the Wounded Feminine. *She also writes for* Commonweal, Worship, Catholic World, *and* Catechumenate. *In addition to having a B.A. from The College of St. Catherine, she has studied in Cologne and at the Jung Institute in Zurich.*

Margaret Nelson *has had careers in nursing and pastoral care, and now has a massage therapy practice. An associate staff member of Loyola Spiritual Resource Center in St. Paul, she is also active in her parish council and RCIA team. She has a B.A. in nursing, an M.A. in Theology, and a Certificate in Pastoral Ministry, all from The College of St. Catherine.*

Anne E. Patrick, *SNJM, a member of the Sisters of the Holy Names, is professor of religion at Carleton College in Northfield, Minnesota, and a recent past president of the Catholic Theological Society of America. She lectures widely on Christian feminist theology and ethics and is currently completing* Conscience and Community: Challenges in Catholic Moral Theology. *Her B.A. and M.A. degrees in English are from Medaille College, Buffalo, New York, and the University of Maryland. She earned two advanced degrees from the University of Chicago: an M.A. in Divinity and a Ph.D. in Religion and Literature.*

Ann Redmond, *CSJ, a Sister of St. Joseph of Carondelet, is professor of English at The College of St. Catherine. Earlier in her career she was involved in elementary education in the Archdiocese of St. Paul-Minneapolis. Her college teaching interests include language, ethics of communication, and literature by women of color. She holds a B.A. from St. Catherine's and M.A. and Ph.D. degrees from the University of Minnesota.*

Elona Street-Stewart, *a Delaware Nanticoke Indian, serves as a community volunteer in areas of racial justice and Native American ministries. Married to an urban pastor, she is also involved in community issues of early childhood and post-secondary educational programs. She has a B.A. in anthropology from Occidental College, Los Angeles.*

Joan H. Timmerman, *professor of theology at The College of St. Catherine, was instrumental in beginning the Theological Insights Program at St. Catherine's. Among her publications are* The Mardi Gras Syndrome: Rethinking Christian Sexuality *(1984) and* Sexuality and Spiritual Growth *(1992). Her B.A., M.A., and Ph.D. degrees are from Marquette University.*

Kay Vander Vort, *together with Joan Timmerman, co-founded the Theological Insights Program. Her career interests include working as a spiritual director at Loyola Spiritual Resource Center in St. Paul and as a member of the training team for spiritual directors at the Wayzata Cenacle. She serves occasionally as an adjunct instructor in theology at The College of St. Catherine. Both her B.A. in theology and English and her M.A. in Theology are from The College of St. Catherine.*

SELECTIONS OF OTHER TITLES FROM
NORTH STAR PRESS OF ST. CLOUD, INC.

Stars in Your Bones

Emerging Signposts on Our Spiritual Journeys *Bozarth, Barkley, Hawthorne*

Through the vibrant art of Julia Barkley, the poetry of Alla Bozarth, and the commentary by Terri Hawthorne, *Stars in Your Bones* journeys through women's spirituality, exploring the wonderful, exciting, and painful stages along the way.

Women of Faith

Portraits of Twelve Spirit-Filled Women *Grace Stageberg Swenson*

Grace Swenson profiles the lives of twelve women who have a clear message for women of today: it is time to reclaim our history, to draw women's stories from the past that will give us a basis to understand ourselves today and plan our futures.

Proud Donkey of Schaerbeek:

Ade Bethune, Catholic Worker Artist *Judith Stoughton*

Ade Bethune, a Belgian immigrant, made unique contributions to the field of sacred art and architecture as an artist, writer, and liturgical consultant. Her leadership spans more than half a century of significant work, all flowing from her early association with Dorothy Day and the publication of her pictures in *The Catholic Worker*.

The Wild Gardener:

The Life and Selected Writings of Eloise Butler *Martha Hellander*

Eloise Butler, a Victorian plant hunter, showed us a life of determination and conviction as she carried out her studies of plants even when women could only be called "amateurs" in science, and she left us a legacy that, nearly sixty years after her death, we can still enjoy.

Grieving: An Inward Journey *Dorothy Samuel*

Dorothy Samuel found healing for the pain caused by her husband's death through an inward journey. With eloquence and insight, the account of this woman's journey and spiritual growth can offer comfort and hope to others who now walk alone.

Stories of the Journey
in the Circle of Life *Kathy St. John Anderson*

Drawing on her Native-American heritage, Kathy Anderson bridges the gap between our daily lives and the larger, natural world. Her stories, in a gentle and affirming way, reconnect us with ourselves and others on the journey of life.